Love Heals Hearts

Transform Your Relationship

By

Mishael Patton
and
W. Craig Patton

AuthorHouse™
1663 Liberty Drive
Bloomington, IN 47403
www.authorhouse.com
Phone: 1-800-839-8640

First published by AuthorHouse 4/12/2010

ISBN: 978-1-4490-1549-7 (e)
ISBN: 978-1-4490-1547-3 (sc)
ISBN: 978-1-4490-1548-0 (hc)

Library of Congress Control Number: 2009912171

Printed in the United States of America
Bloomington, Indiana

This book is printed on acid-free paper.

Dedication

To my husband, Craig,
who inspires and encourages me
to be the best that I can be.

To my wife, Mishael,
who brings joy to my life
and makes me feel complete.

To friends and family
that were instrumental in bringing us together
and creating this beautiful love story.

Love Is

"Love is an amazing thing!
The sun shines brighter,
It makes me want to sing!

I am much mightier,
I feel like a Queen.

He gave me a ring!
I'm so happy, I seem lighter.
Love is an amazing thing!"

--Mishael Patton

Contents

Acknowledgements

• Craig Acknowledges:

Gil Gfelner, a long-time friend and co-worker who suggested I buy a boat and live in Marina del Rey which started the boating chapter of my life.

Eric Olson, a friend at Delta Airlines who introduced me to his sister, Kristen.

Kristen Olson, a good friend who initiated the Catalina Island trip with her friends.

Randy West, my Supervisor at Delta Airlines who allowed me time off each week to fly to San Francisco during our courtship.

Bob Estes, my dock neighbor who let me bend his ear, with my excitement about meeting Mishael, and encouraged me to move forward.

Andy Weintraub, my long-time Shakedown Cruise boating buddy who helped me get the boat ready for the historic September 1990 Catalina Island trip.

My mother, Gloria Fitzgerald, who loved me with all of her heart and made me the man I am today.

My father, Bill Patton, whose life ended much too soon. I miss you and I love you.

My children, Craig Patton, Jr. and Jennifer Lindsay, whom I love dearly and who shared my enthusiasm for my adventure into a new relationship and marriage.

My younger sister, Sherri Barnes, who immediately realized how happy I was, introduced me to her jeweler, and helped me design Mishael's engagement ring.

Tom and Edna Fallen who loved the how-we-met story and encouraged us to write a book and share our love story.

The many flight attendants, shuttle bus drivers, Pink Flamingo Hotel bartenders, and people in the boating community, that had great interest in hearing regular updates of our unfolding love story.

• *Mishael Acknowledges:*

Denise Arndt, who introduced me to Landmark Education, where I became aware that I am a powerful woman and can accomplish outrageous goals like being an Author and living the life of my dreams.

Nancy Lee, Intuitive Psychotherapist, www.nancylee.net, who confirmed the importance of writing the how-we-met story and moving forward with my career as an Author and Speaker.

Gail (Smith) Ben-Zion, my Office Manager at O'Brien, Watters, Davis, Malisch & Piasta, who invited me to a dinner party from which our women's group, the Adventurous Women's Club, was formed.

My mother, Bonnie Bowser, whose tremendous love and support made this book possible.

My father, Bob Bowser, who loved me without conditions.

My son, Lance Clifton, who joined forces with Craig to lovingly tease me incessantly and was very supportive of our relationship commitment.

Carol Stephens, my cousin, who orchestrated a Thanksgiving family get-together so my immediate family could meet Craig.

Kenda Cook, my long-time friend, who was my cheerleader from the inception of this book idea until the final chapter was written.

Ann McIndoo, our Author's Coach, www.SoYouWantToWrite.com, who guided us through the creative process of getting our story out of our heads, onto paper and into your hands.

Introduction

"From every human being there rises a light
that reaches straight to heaven.
And when two souls that are destined to be together
find each other,
their streams of light flow together,
and a single brighter light goes forth from
their united being."
--Author Unknown

• Mishael

Craig and I have been together for two decades and we continue to be extremely happy. We always say, "We're still honeymooning!" When we look at other couples, it is obvious that they don't come close to the level of satisfaction and happiness that we share. We know that we are very fortunate.

We see many unhappy couples that stay together because of their children, for financial reasons, because of habit or convenience, fear of being single, or because they are not confident enough to stand up for themselves and get out of a bad situation. Through the years, we have seen friends and family trying to make challenging, or impossible, relationships work. This is not a good strategy.

When we met we could have easily said no to our relationship because Craig lived in Marina del Rey, in southern California, and I lived many miles north in Calistoga in central California. In spite of some challenges, we both recognized some very special possibilities and decided to move forward. Through the years our love has expanded and our relationship has gotten better and better. We have grown, evolved, become closer, and our relationship has become much stronger, rather than growing apart and in different directions, which is what we see all around us.

We believe that a large part of our relationship success is because we are a perfect, made-in-heaven, meant-to-be match. We do not work hard to make our relationship work; it works with ease for a variety of reasons we will share in the following pages.

In some ways, it feels as though we are like twins. Frequently we think of the same thing, have the same observation and speak or comment in the same way, often at the same time. In other ways, we are opposites. Craig is extroverted, I am introverted. Craig is funny and I am usually quite serious. (However, I am taking lessons from Craig and becoming quite funny.) Craig likes active activities, I generally like quiet activities. We bring the best out in each other; Craig pulls me out for social activities and I bring Craig in for quiet, reflective activities. In our case, opposites do attract.

Craig has told the how-we met story hundreds of times. As time allows, he has the mini version, the short version, the medium-length version, and the full-on long version, which takes several hours. People love to hear our story; they often sit on the edge of their chairs and can't seem to get enough. Through the years we have been encouraged, by many people, to write and share our story.

Because of the intensity of our love, we have noticed that people like being around us. Science has proven that, on one level, everything is energy. We think people feel our love energy, like it and want to create love energy in their own lives. We believe that the energy of love is healing and transformative; therefore, the name, "Love Heals Hearts".

The world needs love. For this reason, we have decided to take our story public. We are on a quest to share our story and help others achieve, in their relationships, the extreme level of satisfaction and love that we share.

We treasure our relationship and are always seeking ways to take good care of each other and find ways to show our love and affection. In later chapters we have included some love strategies that have helped us build the foundation for our successful relationship.

We truly believe that everyone deserves the ultimate happiness of a loving relationship. We hope that our story will provide inspiration, hope and avenues for you to create a passionate and loving relationship in your life.

Prologue

*"I never knew love could mean so much
and get better and better each and every day."
--Craig Patton*

• Craig

I was born in 1947, a baby boomer raised in Manhattan Beach, California. I grew up a beach boy and did a lot of surfing and sailing. I went to Mira Costa High School, played football and sang in a band with my brother, Kirk, and several high school friends. The band was first called Bay Sounds, Inc., we later changed the name to the Wallabies. In the early 1960's our band played at Live Oak Park in Manhattan Beach, the Marina Club in Redondo Beach and Darby Park in Inglewood. In 1965, when I graduated from high school, I worked for General Telephone as a Central Office Installer in West Los Angeles.

In August of 1966 I was drafted into the Army. I spent a year in the states, at Fort Ord in California, Fort Huachuca in Arizona, Fort Lewis in Washington and then found myself on my way to the Central Highlands, in Vietnam, and was there for a year during the Tet Offensive. It was definitely not a fun time but thank goodness I got through it and, in August 1968, I made it home.

I took a couple months to recoup and one day I ran into a friend at the beach and I mentioned that I was looking for work. He told me Delta Airlines was hiring and I thought that could be a great opportunity, so I joined the workforce of Delta Airlines in October of 1968 and I worked there for nearly 31 years.

I got married in 1969 and continued to live in Manhattan Beach. In 1970 William Craig, Jr. was born and in 1972, Jennifer Christine was born. The kids were wonderful and it was fantastic having a boy and a girl. We loved the ocean; my children grew up at the beach. In 1980 I went through a difficult divorce. After my divorce, I lived in Redondo Beach, and in 1982 I moved further south, into a beach cottage overlooking the ocean, in San Clemente. The kids loved taking the train to San Clemente for visits.

As much as I loved living in San Clemente, the commute was tough, over an hour one-way. One night I almost fell asleep and began to drift off the freeway. My friend, Gil, who owned a sailboat in Marina del Rey, knew I was driving too far to work and spending too many hours on the road. He suggested that I consider buying a sailboat and live onboard in Marina del Rey. The lights, bells and whistles went off in my head. My kids would love that, I would love it and the marina was only ten minutes from the airport.

Within a few weeks, in the spring of 1983, I bought a sailboat and moved onboard. I named the boat Moonshadow. I loved the marina community of friends and quickly became known as "The Mayor" of my dock.

Andy had a boat, next to mine, and we became really good friends. One day Andy said, "Craig, you have a new boat, why don't we take a trip to Catalina Island? We'll shake-down the boats and make sure everything is working properly for the season, so when we take family and friends to the island, we will be certain the boats are in tip top shape. We'll call it the Shake-Down Cruise."

Thereafter, every spring we had a Shake-Down Cruise to Catalina Island. It was a guys-only trip, no women or children allowed. We always took lobster, shrimp and clams, partied and had a great time. Through the years, the Shake-Down Cruise was an annual event that we planned for months in advance and looked forward to. Andy had t-shirts made up to commemorate each year's trip.

I continued working at Delta and living on my boat was a lot of fun. In 1987 I often met Eric, a friend that I worked with, at Critters, a restaurant and bar in Hermosa Beach for Happy

Hour and dinner. One time Eric brought his sister, Kristen. Eric thought maybe Kristen and I would like each other and become an item.

Kristen and I didn't make a love connection, but we became very good friends. Kristen would often bring her girlfriends to the marina with food and beverages and we would go sailing. That went on for several years but eventually Kristen moved to the wine country, in Santa Rosa, north of San Francisco.

In the summer of 1990, Kristen called and asked if I would consider taking her and a couple of her friends to Catalina Island. A couple means two, right? I figured that meant her and two of her women friends, so I said okay. About a week later Kristen called and asked if she could add a few more friends to the Catalina Island trip.

I said, "What's a few more?"

She said, "Actually it would be me and six other women."

Right then I nearly lost all of what hair I had left. But, I had a lot of single buddies with sailboats, so I called a meeting with all of my friends to see if they wanted to go with me on a Catalina Island trip with seven single women. We used to invite people down to the marina and have dock parties so I thought these guys would be excited about a Catalina Island trip with women from central California, no problem, right?

All of my boating buddies thought I was out of my mind, they said I was crazy for even considering such a trip. "Those women don't know anything about sailing. You're going to have seasick women on your boat. They are going to be whining all the way over and all the way back!"

I contemplated how we could work out sleeping arrangements if I took all seven women on my boat. With two sleeping in the cockpit, my 30 foot boat could sleep eight. Being the brave person that I am, I was willing to give it a try. I figured that if these women wanted to come down for the trip, I would make sure they had a great time and I would prove to my boating buddies that they had literally "missed the boat". I called Kristen and told her to start planning the trip. And so our story begins.

> *"Love is miraculous and changes everything!"*
> *--Mishael Patton*

• *Mishael*

I was born in 1950 in Tulare, California and did my growing up in the Eugene, Oregon area. I graduated from Henry D. Sheldon High School in 1968, and after one year of college, at the University of Oregon, I became pregnant, got married and my son, Lance Douglas Clifton, was born in 1970. In 1980 I divorced, and in 1986 Lance moved to live with his father. Later that same year I moved to Bend, Oregon and in 1989 I moved to Calistoga, California. This is where our story begins.

In the spring of 1990, Gail, the Office Manager at the law firm where I worked as a Legal Records Manager in Santa Rosa, invited me to a dinner party with her women friends. I was relatively new to the community and didn't know many people, so this was a great opportunity for me to develop new friendships.

Gail served beautifully prepared gourmet food and wine with dinner. It was a diverse group of women and Gail's dining room was a wonderful setting for conversation; we immediately made great connections. We had such a good time that we didn't want the evening come to an end. So, we decided to continue to have dinner parties and set up a rotation schedule with a different hostess and location each month.

After several months of great food and fabulous conversation, it occurred to us that it might be fun to invite some of our men friends. We began inviting our male friends to our dinner parties and the parties became even livelier.

As our dinner parties continued to be fantastic, we thought that it might be even more fun to participate, as a group, in some adventurous activities. We talked about going horseback riding, doing white water rafting trips and various other trips and travels.

We began to refer to ourselves as the Adventurous Women's Club (AWC). When we went places, it was a great conversation starter when someone asked about our group. My response was always, "We're the Adventurous Women's Club, the AWC, we do adventurous activities together," and the conversation would take off from there.

Kristen had been sailing with a friend of hers, in southern California. He had told her about trips to Catalina Island and Kristen came up with the idea that maybe her friend, Craig, would take us to Catalina Island for our first adventurous activity. Everyone liked the idea so, at our next dinner party, Kristen called Craig and asked if he would take her and some of her women friends to Catalina Island.

After we had the trip set up, we had a list of questions about what to bring and at one of our dinner parties I was voted as the one to call Craig and get all of our questions answered. On the telephone he seemed nice enough.

Chapter One
How We Met

"The best and most beautiful things in the world
cannot be seen or even touched.
They must be felt with the heart."
--Helen Keller

<u>**Thursday, September 13, 1990**</u>

• *Mishael*

Since Trudy had a van, Gail, Kathleen, Kristen, Estela and I met at Trudy's house and we drove together to the airport, in Oakland, to catch our flight to Los Angeles.

Oakland Airport waiting for our flight. Left to right around the table:
Trudy, Estela, Kathleen, Mishael, Gail and Kristen

Bev was flying in from back East and would meet us at the airport in Los Angeles. During our flight we had a great time, there was lots of laughter and fun and a few cocktails were consumed.

Flight from Oakland to Los Angeles. Trudy, Mishael and Estela

Across the aisle: Kristen, Kathleen and Gail

When we landed, I was the last one off the plane. I looked out and saw two guys waiting at the gate. One was dressed in jeans, a Hawaiian shirt and a hat, he was tan with the look of a southern California beach boy. The other guy was dressed in a suit.

• *Craig*

This was an exciting day because I was going to meet Kristen and six of her friends. Kristen could party so I knew we would have a great weekend but when I got to the airport that evening I was anxious.

Kristen and I had arranged a limo for transportation to her mom's house, their destination for the night. I ran into the driver so we waited together at the gate. When the plane landed, I knew they were on their way to the gate and I became even more anxious and excited. I wanted to make sure these ladies had an awesome Catalina Island experience.

When the gate opened and people started coming off the plane, I began to identify my crew. They each carried a sleeping bag and an overnight bag. Kristen had said, "You might like one of these women." I was not looking for love, just a good time, but I'm no fool; I was definitely looking them over and checking them out one by one.

Mishael was the last one off the plane and when I saw her she looked familiar to me; it felt like I knew her. (She actually looked like she could be my cousin Liz's twin sister.) She was cute and petite and I remember thinking, *I could like somebody like that.* I was immediately impressed with Mishael as she came over and stood next to me, which gave us a chance to make eye contact. There was a feeling of magnetism that overcame and surrounded me; I felt a little dizzy and was somewhat confused by my feelings.

Mishael made a comment that made me wonder if she really was single and available. We took photos before they jumped into the limo. I followed them to Kristen's mom's house and we visited and made our plans for the weekend. Right off the bat, I felt comfortable with all of the women. I knew they were going to be a great crew.

• *Mishael*

As it turned out, Kristen and Craig had made transportation arrangements for us and the guy in the suit was our limo driver. The other guy, in jeans, was Kristen's friend, Craig.

Standing next to Craig, I felt a bit mesmerized but could not make sense of it. I fleetingly made eye contact with him, but for some reason I was nervous and quickly averted my eyes.

While we were waiting for some of the gals, Craig said, "You should call yourselves the Available Women's Club."

My immediate response was, "No way! That would suggest that we are needy," which caused everyone to laugh.

Curbside, the limo was waiting for us. We took photos in front of the white limo and drank champagne on the drive to Kristen's mom's house in Manhattan Beach.

A limo was waiting for us. Mishael, Kristen, Estela and Trudy

Gail, Kristen and Trudy with the limo driver

Champagne to celebrate. Bev, Mishael and Kristen

Fun in the limo. Trudy, Kathleen and Gail

Craig followed the limo and met us there. We made plans with the limo driver to pick us up the next morning and take us to the marina and we visited with Craig.

That night we made a grocery list and two gals went off to do our shopping for the weekend. Later that night, nude in the hot tub, we agreed that we were all quite impressed with Craig. We fondly began calling him "Captain", since he was the Captain of our boat and our tour guide for the weekend.

Several of the gals had some moderately serious guy friends and I was the only one that was totally unattached and available. So, during our hot tub conversations, it was determined that I could have the Captain for the weekend.

• *Craig*

After I left the AWC women in Manhattan Beach, I went back to the boat and I was as nervous as a long-tailed cat in a room full of rocking chairs. Had I made a mistake? Could I possibly have a successful trip with seven women who had no sailing experience?

<u>Friday September 14, 1990</u>

• *Mishael*

We got up, had breakfast and were getting ready to go. Bev had an accident with a kitchen knife and she had a fairly serious cut on her hand, not a good way to start the weekend. I called Craig to determine if he had sufficient medical supplies onboard or if we should make a stop to get first aid supplies. Craig said he had everything we would need in his medical supply kit.

The limo picked us up and we arrived at the dock with our overnight bags, sleeping bags and groceries. While we loaded the boat and secured everything onboard, we were able to get a really good look at Craig in his fluorescent pink swim trunks and black tank top. He was looking really good. Everything we had agreed on the night before in the hot tub, about me having the Captain for the weekend, was called off. The Captain was now fair game and available to any one of us.

• *Craig*

I got up very early the next morning and did my final check to make sure the boat was ready, the sails were uncovered, and the water tank was full.

I don't know why I was so anxious but when the limo pulled up, my heart was pounding. I was relieved to see they were all wearing sensible shoes and boating attire.

In the marina, on the dock
Top Row: Trudy, Kathleen, Kristen, limo driver, Mishael and Bev
Kneeling: Estela, Gail and Craig

Once the gals came down the dock and I saw the volume of what they were bringing, I thought, *Holy mackerel, we're only going for three days and two nights*, but then I realized they were bringing lots of groceries, which ended up working out perfectly.

We figured out our sleeping arrangements. Gail and Kathleen would sleep in the v-birth, Estela and Mishael would sleep in the settee bunk, Trudy would sleep in the side bench bunk, I would sleep in the quarter birth and Kristen and Bev would take the under-the-stars quarters on the benches in the cockpit.

When the boat was loaded with all of the ladies onboard, I fired up the engine and we left the dock at about 9:30. I had a tape deck and we sang oldies as we headed out of the marina. It was a warm morning, the sky was blue, the ocean was flat and it was an ideal day, except that there wasn't much wind, so we had to motor sail.

On our way to Catalina! Estela, Mishael, Captain Craig and Gail

Kristen was having lots of fun. She began playing matchmaker, and asked me what I thought of Mishael and I said, "She's cute." I had autopilot on the boat so it gave me a chance to visit with all of the ladies and make sure they were comfortable and had everything they needed. I wanted to be certain no one was going to get seasick. Fortunately, prior to the trip they had invested in a patch that goes behind the ear and helps to prevent seasickness. I visited with each of them and got to know their personalities as we motored across the Pacific.

Kristen was a long-time friend and always the life of the party. Gail was a business professional, a gourmet cook and had beautiful long legs. Kathleen was tall and beautiful, with a sparkly personality and was quick to laugh. Trudy was intelligent, caring, very artistic and somewhat reserved. Estela was very laid-back, a reader and appeared to be very introspective. Bev was Kristen's friend from back East and she seemed to be Kristen's opposite, calm, peaceful and tranquil but at the same time a lot of fun. Mishael was quiet, she seemed almost shy, but she was petite and adorable. It was a very enjoyable six hour trip as I visited with my crew.

• *Mishael*

I had never been out in the Pacific Ocean; so for me this was an extreme and almost surreal adventure. From Marina del Rey to Catalina Island, you cross two shipping lanes, highways for the big freighters and container ships. Being so small in such a vast expanse of water, helps adjust perspective regarding our place in the Universe. The weather was beautiful, it was warm and sunny and I was having a great time.

Captain Craig was a good sailor; we felt safe and taken care of

It was a beautiful day for sailing. Kathleen, Mishael, Gail and Kristen

We had a magical moment. We saw dolphin! The dolphin were very playful and seemed to perform for us, diving in and out of the wake of the boat. Craig said that seeing dolphin did not happen very often. We were ecstatic with excitement and felt blessed to see these beautiful creatures. The AWC's first adventurous activity was filled with adventure and at the same time was joyful and relaxing.

• *Craig*

The trip over was peaceful and uneventful. I was so happy that no one got sick or did any whining. My guy friends had been so wrong about these women. The weather could not have been better. We were right on course and right on schedule; it took us six hours to make the crossing to Catalina Island. We went to the Isthmus, in the center of the island, which is the narrowest point of the island, about a quarter of a mile from the east side to the west side.

Just past Bird Rock, as we pulled into Two Harbors, we were met by Harbor Patrol to assign us a mooring for the weekend. My crew was lined up on the side of the boat and looking good with their hair blowing in the wind. The Harbor Master motored up beside our boat, greeted us and asked all of the routine questions like, "How long is your boat?" and "How long will you be staying?"

I said, "The boat is 30 feet and we would like to get a mooring for Friday and Saturday nights. We'll be heading out Sunday morning around 9:00."

He said, "It's a busy weekend. It's Pirate Days this weekend and there are several other events going on as well. I can put you up for tonight, but I will probably have to pull you off the mooring Saturday morning and you will have to hover until I can find another mooring for you."

This made me nervous! Hover means you have to wait for a mooring, and there was no telling how long we would have to wait. And, if we didn't get another mooring on Saturday morning, we would have to go to Descanso Bay and drop an anchor. If that happened, it was certain I would have sick women on my boat. Often in Descanso Bay, there are large swells that cause extreme rocking and rolling of the boat. These women were not prepared for that. I had been in that situation before and it was definitely not fun. I wanted to make sure these women would have a great weekend. I became very bold, took a chance, and said, "Man, I've got seven women on this boat, this is their first time to sail, they have never been to Catalina Island, they are all single and they're ready to party!"

The Harbor Master's boat was rocking back and forth in the wind, and with a big grin on his face, he started thumbing through his clip board, ran his finger down a page and said, "Boy, have I got a mooring for you!" He made a call on his radio, had an employee move his boat and said, "No problem, you will be on a mooring right near the pier for the entire weekend."

For seven years I had been taking my boat to Catalina Island, many times every summer, and this did not ever happen; this was incredible. I guess having seven women onboard, all single and ready to party, tipped the scales in our favor and perhaps interested the Harbor Master as well.

Hooking up to a mooring in the wind can be a challenge; this was another nervous time for me. I asked the ladies to stay out of the way as we worked our way to the mooring. Since Kristen had some experience on the boat, I asked her to grab the stick and pull the mooring line onboard; she did a great job. Once the boat was secured to the mooring, I went to the back of the boat, threw off my hat and dove into the harbor. Boy did that feel good; the cool water calmed me down. Now it was time to celebrate our safe crossing, and begin the party with some food and beverage.

I had talked to Kristen before we left on the trip, to make sure all of the women liked seafood. I knew of a seafood deli in Marina del Rey where we usually got double-clawed live Maine lobsters, shrimp and button clams for our Shake-Down Cruises. I thought seafood would be an excellent plan for this trip, so I snuck onboard eight live Maine lobsters and shrimp on skewers. This was sure to impress my crew and guarantee an enjoyable way to start the weekend.

• *Mishael*

When Craig took his hat off and dove into the water, I noticed that he didn't have very much hair. I made a conscious decision, right then and there, that hair was not an issue for me. I was starting to experience some feelings about the Captain and didn't know why. I was having a small battle in my mind, because I could not justify or make sense of the good feelings I was having about Craig.

• *Craig*

The ladies were sitting in the cockpit enjoying the warm weather and the incredible view of the island. After I got out of the water and dried off, I went down into the galley and grabbed a couple of lobsters. I stood on the stairs leading up to the cockpit with a lobster in each hand and said, "Look what I've got for us!" The ladies were surprised and ecstatic.

To get things rolling, I asked Kristen to start the barbecue and then I handed out skewers of shrimp. That really set the ladies off with ooohs and aaahs; they thought that was awesome. Kristen was managing the shrimp on the barbecue while I cooked the lobster. I handed out plates of lobster for them to share.

While we ate shrimp and lobster, I kept watching Mishael and I thought, *This girl's cute*, and I kind of liked her. We threw the shells and leftovers into the ocean and that brought a lot of fish around the boat. The water was very clear and we watched the beautiful orange Garibaldi and dozens of beautiful fish swimming around the boat. The seafood surprise was a great success.

As the evening progressed, I told them that we could call the Shore Boat to pick them up and take them to shore so they could shower and get ready for the evening. There would be a live band at Doug's Harbor Reef where they have food, music, an outdoor bar and a dance floor. They were excited as they anticipated a fun evening. After we finished eating, I began cleaning up in the galley and I noticed Mishael came down the stairs and into the boat.

She walked right past me, disappeared, and I had no idea where she went. I stopped working, looked around and saw her lying on the bunk. I thought, *Oh, no, she must be sick.* I began thinking something must have been wrong with the seafood and wondered how many others would be coming downstairs to lie down. I might have sick women on the boat after all. I looked at Mishael, she was lying on her back with her hands behind her head and she had a big smile on her face. I asked, "Are you okay?"

• *Mishael*

I said, "I'm excellent!" There was an innuendo there and I hoped he got it. I was wondering how he could possibly notice me among the six other women.

• *Craig*

She was excellent alright! I called on the radio for the Shore Boat to come pick up the ladies. They all scurried downstairs to grab their bags as I continued cleaning the galley.

• *Mishael*

For reasons I could not explain, I was developing a fondness for Craig. I felt confused because I didn't know him well enough to feel good about him but warm and tingly feelings persisted. I wanted to stay on the boat and go ashore with the Captain but the women were expecting me to go to shore with them. Although I wanted to stay with the Captain; first, I didn't know if Craig would want me to stay with him and second, I didn't know how to make that happen.

The Shore Boat was waiting and the gals were saying, "Come on Mishael, let's go!" Staying with the Captain simply was not an option. So, I gathered my bag and got ready to go. As I walked by Craig, something overcame me and I did something totally out of character that I did not intend to do.

I leaned over to Craig, who was still cleaning the galley, and held his face in my hands and gave him a small kiss…right on the lips!

As I drew back, still holding his face in my hands, I looked him in the eyes and said, "You are coming dancing aren't you?"

As I stepped on the Shore Boat I was thinking, *Wait!! Stop!!! What just happened? Did I kiss someone I don't even know? Where did that come from? I'm shy, quiet and careful. Have I lost my mind? What's up with me?*

• *Craig*

Wow!!! Sparks were flying!! I was shocked and excited by that kiss. I could hardly speak; somehow I managed to say, "Yes." Damn! Why did the Shore Boat have to show up right then? I started working faster; I had never cleaned the galley so fast. Fortunately, I didn't have to call the Shore Boat, I had towed a dingy, a small inflatable with an outboard motor, behind the Moonshadow. I jumped into the dingy, went to shore, showered, and headed for Doug's Harbor Reef. I knew there would be more men than women at the restaurant, that's the norm for the island, lots of sailing guys and very few women.

When I walked into Doug's Harbor Reef I saw Mishael sitting on a stool and after that surprising kiss in the galley, I thought it would be a good time to respond. My heart was pounding as I slid behind her and put my arms around her.

• *Mishael*

It was a really fun evening at Doug's Harbor Reef. The island atmosphere was exotic and the music was great. When Craig arrived at the outdoor bar and dance floor, he zeroed in on me and we spent the entire evening dancing. We all danced late into the evening and had an incredible time. As it turned out, the Captain was a very good dancer, the kind of dancer that catches everyone's attention and draws a crowd. He was quite a site to behold on the dance floor and was clearly the Dancing King at Doug's Harbor Reef.

• *Craig*

Besides dancing with Mishael, I danced with every woman that would dance. I think some of the guys even wanted to dance with me. It was crazy fun and we danced late into the night. After that kiss on the boat, my arms around Mishael on the stool, dancing with her, laughing and looking into her green eyes; I wanted to take Mishael away from the crowd and the loud music and have her all to myself.

I asked her to join me for a walk on the beach. It was a gorgeous night, the tide was out and the sand was wet, warm and glowing with light from the moon. I can still recall the feeling of my bare feet on the sand. It was a very romantic setting and we walked along the beach for more than an hour.

Everyone else made their way back to the Moonshadow on the Shore Boat, but Mishael and I went back in the dingy. That week there was a red tide, which is caused by algae growth in the water, and any motion in the water caused a phosphorescent green sparkly light. So, when the propeller spun, when fish swam, or when you moved your hand through the water, there were green sparkles in the water and it was absolutely beautiful. Mishael was, needless to say, intrigued and thrilled.

We were not in a hurry to get back to the boat so we cruised around the harbor, took in the sites and enjoyed the red tide and the moonlight shimmering on the water. I didn't think I could top the beach walk, but the dingy ride extended our very romantic evening.

It was quite late when we finally arrived at the boat. All of the other ladies had retired for the evening. We stood astern on the back of the boat, and I pointed out various landmarks on the mainland. We were 33 miles from Marina del Rey but it was so clear we could see planes lined up in the sky waiting to land at Los Angeles International Airport.

Saturday was going to be a big day and we needed to get some sleep; so we decided we had better turn in for the night. We had a difficult time disengaging; Mishael snuggled in with me in the quarter birth and we cuddled the night away.

• *Mishael*

Friday night was spectacular! Dancing, the beach-walk, the late night harbor cruise, cuddling and holding each other throughout the night; my Prince Charming had arrived and I had been swept off my feet!

But wait!! What was happening to me? This was not my typical behavior, usually I was quiet and cautious. Somehow this tropical island ambiance had caused me to be wild and reckless. Had there really been green sparkles in the water? I was confused.

Saturday, September 15, 1990

• *Craig*

On Saturday morning Mishael and I were the first ones up. No one seemed to notice that Mishael didn't sleep in the settee bunk with Estela. It was a beautiful morning in the cockpit, there was no wind, it was warm and the sky was bright blue. Six of the ladies were wearing big t-shirts for sleeping attire. Mishael was wearing the cutest hot pink and purple pajama shorts and top. She was just out of bed with her hair messed up and no makeup on; she looked irresistible. We had coffee, fruit and bagels with conversation and laughter about Friday night at Doug's Harbor Reef.

• *Mishael*

Those pink and purple pajamas were a gift from my mother, if she only knew what I was up to in my pajamas. The next morning in the cockpit, there was much chatter and fun over breakfast. As I observed Craig, I was overwhelmed with feelings of fondness. I did not know him well and could not justify my feelings; I was uncertain and confused so I dismissed my feelings. But, at the same time, I was hoping I could somehow manage some private time with him so we could continue our conversation from last night and get to know each other a little better.

We had planned rest and relaxation on the beach that day. We intended to sun ourselves, read and have lazy conversations. We wanted to be rested for another fun evening of dancing.

• *Craig*

Saturday morning I took my camera and snapped a few pictures; I captured the ladies being leisurely on the beach.

Leisure on the beach. Left to right, Kristen, Bev, Kathleen in front, Trudy, Estela, Gail and Mishael

It was difficult for me to be still and lie around, so I asked Mishael if she would like to go for a walk. It was a pleasant walk up to the Banning House, a historic old bed and breakfast that was built in 1910 for the Banning brothers who owned Catalina Island at that time. From the patio at the Banning House, to the east we could see the mainland and Two Harbors, where my boat was moored, and to the west we could see Cat Harbor.

I wanted to get to know Mishael and I wanted her to know me. I wanted to tell her about my children and I wanted to know about her family. We talked about everything non-stop. Looking into her green eyes was stirring up some feelings; I was not sure exactly what was going on but I knew in my heart that something spectacular was happening.

While we were sitting there we saw people in pirate costumes on a treasure hunt. And, we also saw dozens of sailboats, with beautiful multi-colored sails, tacking back and forth on a bright blue sea as they came toward the island. Later when we walked back to the beach, we saw 75 catamarans lined up on the beach. It was a beautiful sight.

Catamarans on the beach

We joined the women on the beach and went back to the boat to gather our groceries and get ready for the evening. Later we came back to the beach and secured a barbecue fire pit near the pier. We had an excellent seafood dinner as the sun was setting. We all laughed, teased and had a great time.

As we looked down the beach, we saw the guys from the catamarans having their barbecue. There was not one woman in their group. There were 300 eyes looking at me, with my crew of seven women, and I am sure they wondered why I was such a lucky guy. As the night went on, a lot of those guys began filtering down the beach and started chatting with the AWC women.

• *Mishael*

That night on the beach we put together a wonderful dinner party, we barbecued a variety of fish and made a big salad; we were definitely well-fed. It was a beautiful, warm, starlit night on the beach.

There were two men on each of those 75 catamarans that we saw coming into the island earlier in the afternoon. That meant 150 men just down the beach from us who were checking us out pretty heavily. During the evening they looked at us and we looked at them. Later the catamaran boys came down our way, around our fire pit, and started visiting, talking and getting to know some of us gals. One of the men started talking with me and I immediately knew I had no interest. To my surprise, I grabbed Craig's arm and said, 'I'm with the Captain!" Once again, I didn't plan to say that, I did not mean to say that and I did not know where that came from. I surprised myself and everyone that heard my bold statement.

• *Craig*

When Mishael grabbed my arm and said, 'I'm with the Captain,' that made me feel special; it made my heart sing to know that she had feelings for me. I knew something extraordinary was happening. In the midst of feeling good, I was also confused. I had no intention of getting involved with anybody, but I could feel myself going through some changes.

Earlier in the trip I had mentioned that on Sunday morning, we had to leave the harbor no later than 9:00 a.m. in order to make it back to Marina del Rey, so they could get to the airport in time to catch their evening flight. Once again on

Saturday night I said, "Without fail, you all have to be onboard Moonshadow when we depart at 9:00 a.m. If not, you'll have to take the Express Boat back to the mainland and most likely you'll miss your flight."

Later that evening we cleaned up and organized. I told the ladies to go on to Doug's Harbor Reef and I would take everything to the boat and meet them on the dance floor. I couldn't wait to get back to Doug's Harbor Reef, because I knew it would be entertaining watching all those guys hovering around the AWC women. I wasn't let down, it was an awesome evening; everybody danced and had a good time. Much later we headed back to the boat for sleep. It seemed the weekend had gone by way too quickly.

• *Mishael*

Saturday night Craig was a lot of fun; we danced and danced and laughed and laughed. I don't recall ever having so much fun. I felt intoxicated with joy; it seemed as though I was in a romantic whirlwind that was spinning me round and round.

<u>Sunday, September 16, 1990</u>

• *Craig*

Sunday morning everybody was climbing out of their bunks except two; we were missing Kristen and Kathleen. Obviously, they were having such a great time; they didn't make it back to the boat. I was nervous, the clock was ticking and we needed to leave on time.

Shortly before 9:00 a.m. I was looking toward shore and all of a sudden I saw Kristen and Kathleen waving from the pier. They were yelling, "We're here, don't leave without us, we'll be right there." Thank goodness! Everybody on the boat was cheering and clapping. We had no idea where those two had been and we didn't care, just as long as they made it back to the boat.

I had the engine running when the Shore Boat delivered Kristen and Kathleen, and we were ready to roll; we left the island on time. Heading out of the harbor, I needed somebody to steer the boat while I prepared the sails for the trip. I asked Mishael to steer the boat.

• *Mishael*

He chose me to steer the boat! I felt proud, privileged and special. I was feeling pretty happy about my weekend. The trip back was uneventful, the weather was spectacular and I loved being out on the ocean. It gave me space and time to be with myself and dreamily review the events of weekend. It was a lovely ocean crossing though I was sad to see the weekend coming to an end.

Craig and I frequently made eye contact and conversed briefly. I was feeling tremendously confused. I didn't know Craig very well. We had spent only a few days together and yes, he appeared to be a nice guy and he was very gracious, friendly and thoughtful. He was a wonderful host and as Captain of our trip, he certainly made sure everyone had a good time and was gentlemanly, kind and conscientious.

I was feeling some pretty big tugs on my heart strings. I couldn't make sense of that, because I had a hard stance with myself regarding moving through life independently. I was confused about what was going on in my heart.

• *Craig*

We had a good trip back to Marina del Rey. I visited with everybody and that was fun. But, something was happening to me, I was unsure what was going on and confused about how I was feeling. I was experiencing a feeling of euphoria that I hadn't felt in many years. All the way across the ocean, Mishael and I made eyes at each other.

We made it back to Marina del Rey with time to spare. My good friend, Bob, who lived on his boat, came over and took pictures. After that we all talked and laughed while we waited for the limo to pick them up.

Back in Marina del Rey tanned and seasoned sailors
Top Row: Kristen and Bev
Middle Row: Estela, Captain Craig, Mishael and Trudy
Kneeling: Kathleen and Gail

I was feeling sad. Mishael and I exchanged phone numbers. When I saw Mishael tear up, I got a lump in my throat. I hadn't had this exhilarating feeling in a long time; it was special and I couldn't believe it.

Later that evening my dock buddies gathered around to hear about the trip and anxiously asked when we were going on the next trip. I had a great time teasing them; I triumphantly told them there wasn't going to be a next trip and that they had literally "missed the boat".

• *Mishael*

It was a sad departure from Marina del Rey. It was Sunday night, we were tired and we all had to get back to work on Monday. Craig had asked me to call him when I got home to make sure I had a safe trip. It was a long trip and it was late when I arrived at home. When I called Craig to tell him I made it home, I dialed his number and it was an invalid number.

I was shocked! I thought maybe we had something special going on, but I guess maybe we didn't. Did Craig give me a wrong number? I began looking at one of the numbers and thought maybe it was an eight instead of a six, so I dialed the number correctly and he answered the phone. I was both excited and anxious to talk but it was a very short conversation. I just said, "We made it back."

And, Craig responded, "I'm glad you had a safe trip. I know you must be tired, so I'll talk with you later."

That was the end of our conversation. Although I was disappointed when I hung up, when I went to sleep that night, I had hope and a feeling that something special was going to happen.

Chapter Two
Courtship

"When I'm with you;
I'm in touch with the beautiful,
loveable and capable parts of me."
--Ken Keyes, Jr.

<u>**Monday, September 17, 1990**</u>

• *Craig*

When I went back to work on Monday morning everyone I worked with was anxious to know about my weekend. Not much work was done that morning, because everybody sat down in a group and I told the story.

Then I started thinking about the night before and how I had cut the conversation off so abruptly. I felt especially bad when she told me that she thought I had given her a wrong number; she may have felt that I wasn't genuine and more importantly, perhaps not interested. I knew I already adored Mishael and I decided I had to show her how much I cared and I wanted her to know I was sorry about the way our phone conversation had ended on Sunday night.

I contacted Kristen to find out Mishael's office address in Santa Rosa, and I talked with my Boss, Randy. I went to a floral shop and told the florist I needed to send flowers to a beautiful woman I had just met. The lady in the store asked about the beautiful woman that was receiving flowers and I gave her a condensed version of the how-we-met story; a ten minute visit to the floral shop turned into an hour. We went through her floral book and found a nice bouquet of roses. I said, "Can you make certain these flowers are delivered today?"

And she said, "Yes, no problem."

That really excited me, because I knew when Mishael saw these flowers, she would know I was thinking about her. I wanted to send flowers to show her how much I cared. I'm not sure what time it was when we talked on Sunday night, but it was late and I was tired. I was nervous and trying to sort out what was happening and I didn't want to say anything foolish; I wanted to get off the phone as quickly as possible which seemed like the safest thing to do.

I needed time to think about what had happened over the weekend and I wanted to sort out the direction of my future. I needed to think through what to say to her because I wanted to be certain our next conversation would be meaningful and special. I knew that I was already having intense feelings for her so for now, flowers would be a good way to get things started. I did a lot of thinking that night and did not sleep well.

• *Mishael*

It had been an exhilarating and exhausting weekend; I got to bed late and woke up tired. On Monday it was business as usual, just another day at the office. Mid-morning the Receptionist called and said, "Mishael, you'd better come out here."

My response was, "I'm really busy right now, what is it?"

"No, you really have to come out here!"

I was getting annoyed, and again, I said, 'What is it?"

She said, "You have to come and *see* this to believe it!"

I went out to the lobby and there, on the Receptionist's desk, was the most beautiful and extraordinary bouquet of red roses I had ever seen. The bouquet was so large that you could hardly see the Receptionist. The flowers were the talk of the office that day; there was chatter about the flowers and lots of inquiries about who had sent them.

I called Craig to thank him for the flowers later that night. We had a lengthy conversation and I felt comfortable and much better than on Sunday night when our conversation ended so abruptly. At some point during the conversation Craig said, "Maybe in a month of two I could come up for a visit to Calistoga."

Suddenly, it happened again, I said something I didn't plan to say. I said, "I can't wait a month!" I was shocked!!! Again, I couldn't understand where the words came from or why I said them but that was the moment when the momentum shifted. We began making plans for a weekend of fun in Calistoga.

Tuesday, September 18, 1990

• *Craig*

After our conversation, I was excited about seeing Mishael again and I didn't want to wait an entire month to see her. On Tuesday morning, when I went into work, I sat down with my Boss, Randy. He already knew I was enamored with this lady and I explained the situation. At that time Delta had a flight every hour from Los Angeles to San Francisco. I asked Randy if I could take half a day off on Friday and fly out to central California for an extended weekend with Mishael. Randy was excited about my excitement; we agreed that I would bring a suit and take the 1:00 Friday afternoon flight to San Francisco, I would fly back on Monday morning and go right to work. Back in those days, Delta employees were required to wear business suits when we were passengers.

After I got my travel arrangements squared away, my nervousness turned into intense excitement. That night, when I got home, I called Mishael to tell her that I had made arrangements to fly up on Friday. She was thrilled and we had a nice conversation. Our plan was that I would fly to San Francisco on Friday, take the fly-away bus to the Pink Flamingo Hotel, in

Santa Rosa, Mishael would pick me up that evening after work and we would begin our weekend.

Wednesday, September 19, 1990

• *Mishael*

I was so excited he was coming to see me! I began my weekend preparation by doing a survey, with all my friends and co-workers, to determine the most fantastic and romantic restaurant in the area. After several days of research and survey, I decided on the restaurant at the Chateau Sovereign Winery near Healdsburg, a few miles north of Santa Rosa.

My second concern was wardrobe selection…what would I wear? The only thing Craig had seen me wearing was weekend casual clothes, and of course, those hot pink pajamas. My goal was to knock his socks off when he saw me; I wanted to look my absolute best! I chose a long floral dress, with a short jacket, that I had purchased for a friend's August wedding in Oregon. It was a great dress and I knew I looked fantastic in it.

Thursday, September 20, 1990

• *Craig*

Of course, Mishael and I spoke on Thursday night and we discussed our weekend plans. Again, I didn't sleep well because I was so excited about flying out on Friday to see her.

<u>Friday, September 21, 1990</u>

• *Mishael*

On Friday my feet didn't touch the ground. I was so excited I floated around all day and didn't accomplish much work at the office. I was experiencing such an intense feeling of anticipation, I was short of breath and it felt like my heart was going to burst out of my chest. It was like when you're at the beginning of a roller coaster ride, slowly going up and anticipating the excitement of the ride. It was a feeling of exhilaration that I came to enjoy often.

• *Craig*

I got dressed in my suit and tie, went up to the gate and waited for the flight; I lucked out, I was the only one in First Class and I knew the Flight Attendant, Candy. She asked me why I was going to San Francisco. She became engrossed in my story and, since I was the only one in her area, she sat next to me and we talked for an entire hour. It was fun to tell her the story and it added to my excitement and anticipation.

I departed the plane and the fly-away bus to Santa Rosa arrived in the terminal. I stepped onto the bus and the only seat available was right behind the Driver.

When I sat down, he said, "Where are you going?"

"I'm going to the Pink Flamingo Hotel, in Santa Rosa."

"What's in Santa Rosa? Are you going there for business?"

It's about an hour and a half drive, so I ended up telling him the whole story. Narrating the story was, once again, exciting for me. It seemed like every time I told the story I got even more excited and people's reactions confirmed how special our weekend had been.

The Driver said, "Boy, you must have been quite the Skipper!"

Once we reached Santa Rosa and arrived at the hotel; it was early and I knew Mishael would not be arriving until around 5:30. Since I had some time to kill and my nerves were sky-rocketing, I decided to go into the bar and have a glass of wine, hopefully that would calm me down.

The Bartender was a woman and lo and behold, I was the only person in the bar at that time. She said, "So, what brings you to Santa Rosa?"

"Boy, have I got a story for you!" I sat down at the bar and started telling her the story.

She leaned on the bar, with her chin in her palm, kept the wine bottle on the bar and kept my glass full. She thought it was the most amazing story. She said, "You're one lucky man!"

And I said, "No, they were lucky women!"

I didn't want to have too much to drink so I decided to walk around the lobby of the hotel. Once again, my nerves flared up and I began pacing; I feared that I might wear out the carpet. As the clock ticked, I became more nervous as I knew it was getting close to the time that Mishael would be arriving. I went into the Gift Shop and looked around and when I walked out of the Gift Shop, Mishael had arrived and was standing inside the lobby door. The light from the late afternoon sun was coming through a window and shining on her. Time stopped, my heart pounded fiercely and I held my breath. It was a surreal and magical moment which I still remember and see clearly to this day. It was like a slow-motion scene in a movie.

Mishael looked absolutely beautiful! She was wearing a long dress, with pastel flowers on it. We ran to each other. I hugged her, picked her up and swung her around. I needed a moment to catch my breath and soak up the phenomenal feelings I was experiencing.

Shortly after that, we left the hotel and Mishael surprised me by driving to the Chateau Sovereign Winery. We had a dinner reservation, but we had arrived a little early so we wandered around, held hands, and strolled through the beautiful grounds of the winery. When we walked into the dining room, the carpet was so thick; it felt like we were walking on a cloud.

At Chateau Sovereign Winery for dinner

We sat down at the table and it seemed as though we had ten very attentive waiters. We had an elegant and delicious dinner, but the best part was looking across the table and seeing Mishael. I couldn't take my eyes off her! Still, I wondered what was happening to me, my head was spinning, and trust me, the wine had nothing to do with it. Mishael couldn't have picked a more romantic setting for our first evening together in the wine country; it was magnificent!

After dinner we drove to her cottage in Calistoga. It was a beautiful cottage with roses in the flower beds and potted plants on the porch. It felt great to be there. We started a fire in the fireplace. Then I met Raja, a black and white adorable cat that was outdoors all day and came into the cottage at night. The entire evening was wonderful.

• *Mishael*

There was a long driveway through the orchard to the cottage. When Raja saw me drive in he would usually run through the orchard, jump in my arms and I would give him kitty pets for about ten minutes, then he would come into the cottage and we would spend pleasant evenings together.

We had a fabulous relationship, and loved each other dearly. Raja was a little spoiled. At night Raja slept at the foot of the bed, but by morning he was usually on my pillow by my face.

Craig didn't mind Raja on the bed, but a cat on the pillow didn't work for him at all. Raja seemed to think that Craig's pillow was his pillow so this created a bit of an issue. On weekends, when Craig was in town, Prince Raja was demoted to the laundry room at night.

Saturday, September 22, 1990

• *Craig*

It was an absolutely beautiful Saturday morning at the cottage; I loved waking up there. Out of every window all you could see were walnut orchards and vineyards, it was rural and quiet. Mishael prepared a wonderful breakfast in the country-style kitchen.

Earlier in the week, when we were planning the weekend, Mishael said that we might go for a walk, and it would be a good idea to bring hiking boots. When I unpacked my boots, we discovered that we had identical Hi-Tec hiking boots.

From the cottage it was a quarter mile walk to the center of downtown Calistoga so there was no need to take a car. We spent the entire day in Calistoga, population 4,300, exploring the village. We went to the museum, saw Sam Brannon's cottages, watched gliders at the Gliderport, had lunch in a cute restaurant and browsed in book stores and boutiques. I had never been to this area and Mishael was a fantastic tour guide. It was wonderful to stroll, hold hands and look at her. Later we went home, spiffed up a bit, and had dinner out at Mishael's favorite Calistoga restaurant, Pacifico's.

Sunday, September 23, 1990

• *Mishael*

On Sunday we choose at-home time with leisurely rest and relaxation. We also tried to sort out and make sense of what was going on between us. Before the day was over, we had made a promise to each other and to a committed relationship. I was thrilled but scared. We had some hesitation as we both had previous first marriages and we wanted to establish a foundation for relationship success. We talked about what components were necessary for a successful relationship and had lengthy discussions regarding values like honesty and integrity. We talked and read by the fireplace, which was very romantic. I made lentil soup, it was Craig's first lentil experience and he discovered that I was a very good cook.

• *Craig*

Talking about relationships and how we felt eased some of my confusion and nervousness. Mishael was a quality person with high integrity, and my anxieties and trust issues with women were dissolving. I was happy about the commitment we made.

A candlelit bath with Mishael was the topper of the evening. I was used to living on a boat and walking up the docks to the shower facilities, often in the rain or fog. I got so accustomed to that and had forgotten what a bathtub was like. Everything about the Calistoga cottage was incredibly romantic and exciting.

• *Mishael*

The entire weekend was a huge success! My research had paid off; the Friday night restaurant choice at Chateau Sovereign Winery was the perfect beginning of our romantic weekend. There was so much to see and do in Calistoga and it was fun for me to orchestrate our activities. The best part was just being together, we scored very high on being companionable; we were comfortable together and seemed to be a very good match. I was exhilarated and delighted, the weekend was a whirlwind of fun.

Monday morning I took Craig to the Pink Flamingo Hotel to catch the fly-away bus to San Francisco. After he left I missed him and was sad that our weekend went by so quickly.

Courtship Continues

• *Craig*

During my numerous three and four-day weekend visits to Calistoga we did many walks around the village, dined in lots of restaurants and we really enjoyed watching the planes take off and land at the Gliderport. We did Napa and Sonoma Valley wine tours and lots of activities, but what I liked best was sitting in Mishael's backyard. Being a city boy, the quiet rural setting was a totally new experience for me. You could hear the gliders overhead, there was a garden with basil, artichokes and vegetables and we liked walking around in the orchard. It was absolutely beautiful there and I loved every minute of it. Being at the cottage with Mishael was heaven on earth.

• *Mishael*

We continued to find great pleasure in reading by the fireplace. We read out loud to each other from several of Ken Keyes Jr.'s books, he is the Author of *Handbook to Higher Consciousness, The Power of Unconditional Love, Prescriptions for Happiness* and many other books. We latched onto what became our favorite Quote from Ken Keyes, Jr. When asked, "What does love really mean?" Ken replied, "When I'm with you, I'm in touch with the beautiful, lovable and capable parts of me." That became a Quote we thought about and said to each other often, because it truly explained how we were feeling.

In mid-October after a playful and fun-filled weekend, Craig jokingly said, "Will you marry me?"

I jokingly replied, "Of course, I'll marry you;" however, I had no true interest in ever getting married. I thought marriage was only for young people who intended to have children. We both had grown children and no desire for a larger family. I preferred to live happily ever after as a committed couple.

• *Craig*

I shocked myself when I heard myself say, "…marry me". I had no intention of getting married again, but after I said that I began to dream about our future together. Being with Mishael was so right, we were compatible and companionable and I could see myself being married to her. I didn't understand the why of it, but deep down inside I knew we were becoming an awesome couple and I had found somebody I wanted to spend the rest of my life with.

I decided I to follow through with a marriage proposal. My younger sister, Sherri, knew a jeweler and she helped me design a ring for Mishael. In the meantime, I wanted to get some type of promise ring so I went to Don's Jewelers, in

Manhattan Beach. I found a ring with a little chip of a diamond and decided I would propose with that ring while the real engagement ring was being made.

I had to think of a way to present the ring to Mishael, so I got a silly idea and went to Buffum's department store and bought a little stuffed bear named Buffy. I would have him carry the ring, and be the ring "bear-er" which I thought was a clever idea.

By this time, I had made many trips to Calistoga, and each time I had the same flight attendant, the same bus driver and the same bartender at the Pink Flamingo Hotel. Each trip they asked for an update and enjoyed hearing the story of our blossoming romance.

In mid-October, on one of my flights to San Francisco, I had Buffy sitting in the seat next to me in First Class, with a seatbelt on and holding the ring in his lap. Candy, the Flight Attendant, smiled and said, "Is this the day for the big question?"

"This is it, and I brought Buffy along for a little support."

During the flight, Candy had a chance to sit and talk with me. When I departed the plane, she handed me a bottle of champagne and said, "Here, have a toast on me!"

When I got on the bus, the driver saw Buffy and I showed him the ring. He smiled and said, "Go for it, Skipper!"

The same thing happened when I went into the bar at the Pink Flamingo Hotel. The Bartender said, "Who's your friend?"

"He's the ring bear-er."

She looked at me and said, "You're really serious about this woman aren't you?"

"Yes, I've found the woman I want to spend the rest of my life with."

"She's a very lucky woman!"

"No, I'm a very lucky man!"

• *Mishael*

When I picked up Craig, at the Pink Flamingo Hotel that day, he didn't appear to be himself. He seemed nervous and anxious and was pacing around; I wasn't sure what was wrong with him. Then Craig handed me a bear named Buffy and said, "Here, Buffy can keep you company when I'm not here with you."

I said, "Oh, okay," and we left to go to the Hungry Hunter for lunch.

• *Craig*

When we got to the parking lot of the restaurant that day I was really nervous. We started to get out of the car and I said, "Wait!" I looked at her, told her I loved her and that I wanted to spend the rest of my life with her. I presented the promise ring to her and asked her to "marry me and fly free".

• *Mishael*

I was ecstatic about where our relationship was going. I loved the fact that we were building the foundation for a committed re-lationship and now here was a promise ring which put us on an entirely different level of commitment. I did have some resistance to marriage, but Craig was adamant about marriage versus committed relationship. He wanted a wedding with all of our friends and family present and our children in the wedding party. That felt good to me and sealed the deal. A wedding was really about celebration and we certainly had lots of reasons to celebrate.

• *Craig*

It was a peaceful weekend in the cottage in Calistoga. I loved walking around in the orchard and vineyards. One day Mishael said, "Hey, do you like figs?"

I said, "Yes."

And she said, "Come with me."

We walked out through the walnut orchard and, much to my surprise, in the middle of the walnut grove was a huge fig tree. I loved figs and the figs happened to be ripe. Being from the city, this seemed very cool.

We pulled a few figs off the tree and ate them right there. To me, things like that were romantic. When I bit into that fig, it reminded me of my grandfather, Luke Smith. When I was very young, he taught me a way to put your mouth on the fig, squeeze it, and the whole fig would pop right out of the skin and into your mouth. Eating those figs brought back fond childhood memories of pleasant times with my grandfather.

• *Mishael*

I moved to Calistoga in the summer of 1989 and lived there for a year before I met Craig. I was familiar with places to go, things to do and local activities. It is an incredibly beautiful area and having our courtship in the wine country was fantastic. We visited some of the more unique wineries but there was so much more to see and do. We discovered we both liked history.

We visited the darling little town of Sonoma. There is, of course, a winery there and great restaurants. The town is built around a park in the square, the old barracks are still there, as well as General Vallejo's house which was built when California was a Mexican territory. The first citrus trees in California, grapefruit trees, were imported from China and planted at General Vallejo's home.

We also became interested in exploring the Glen Ellen area, which is where Jack London lived. Jack London Park is incredible with remnants of Jack's Wolf House that burned down before it was completed.

In the little town of Glen Ellen we enjoyed the winery and a charming old tavern. We especially liked a used bookstore there with a cat that slept in a basket on the counter. In the back of this bookstore, we met a Jack London Scholar, Russ Kingman, who was putting together a collection of Jack London's books. As it turned out, one of Craig's favorite books, as a young boy, was *Burning Daylight,* by Jack London. After spending an afternoon with Russ Kingman, we had a revived interest in Jack London, started reading many of his books and even secured some of his books that were out of print. We became especially enchanted with *The Valley of the Moon*, an early California romance novel, written in 1913, in which Jack and Charmian London's experiences are mirrored in the central characters, Billy and Saxon, who were living a miserable working class existence in the late 1800's in Oakland, California. They embarked on an epic walking journey in search of prosperity, fulfillment and a dream ranch that they thought could only exist in "a valley on the moon". That referred to the Valley of the Moon in the Glen Elen area, where Jack's ranch was, the book included many local landmarks. We generally became intrigued with the life of Jack and Charmian London and did much reading and research about their travels and sailing adventures.

We also did a lot of exploration in San Francisco. We loved the Golden Gate Park, the Arboretum, the various museums and Japanese Gardens as well as the Exposition and China Town. One weekend we took the ferry to Sausalito, had lunch and ferried back. We also did some hiking on Mt. Tamalpais.

Near St. Helena we went to a historic gristmill and we discovered a Robert Lewis Stevenson Museum. We hiked up to a cabin, north of Calistoga, where Robert Lewis Stevenson wrote *Treasure Island* in a little wooden cabin where he lived with his bride. Everything we did was somehow a romantic activity.

We visited Luther Burbank's home and gardens in Santa Rosa. Luther was a Horticulturalist, Jack London's friend, and among his many activities he sought to develop a cactus, without spines, that could solve world hunger.

We explored the Russian River area. We went to the beach at Jenner. We explored Bodega Bay where the movie, *The Birds* was filmed. We also attended a few Adventurous Women's Club parties. It was an amazing few months packed with many romantic and adventurous activities.

Chapter Three
Family and Friends

"Love is but the discovery of ourselves in others,
and the delight in the recognition."
--Alexander Smith

Grandfather Smith Passed Away

• *Craig*

In the fall, when I was at Mishael's house, I received a call and learned that my Grandfather Smith had passed away which made for a very sad day. I can't think of anybody I would rather have been with when I received the news of his death. Mishael immediately understood how I felt. We talked about life and death, she comforted me and helped me accept the reality that my grandfather had passed away.

• *Mishael*

I remember this moment so clearly. It was early November, we had been together only a month and a half. After Craig hung up the telephone, having just received news that his grandfather had passed away, we hugged and held each other, and swayed to the music. In the background I heard Stevie Wonder singing, "…Heaven is ten zillion light years away…" It felt as though we were cementing our relationship and preparing to support and love each other through both good times and challenging times.

Engagement Party

• *Craig*

In November I got together with Andy, my good friend on the dock, and we planned a dock party. It was to be a combination birthday party for Andy and engagement party for me and Mishael. It would be a great time for all of us to get together and an opportunity to introduce Mishael to my family and friends. I wanted them know her, recognize her good qualities and understand everything I loved about her. I wanted them to comprehend why my heart sang every time I was with her or talked to her on the phone. I was very excited about this dock party.

• *Mishael*

I flew to Los Angeles on Friday, the evening before the engagement party in Marina del Rey. Over dinner I met Craig's sister, Sherri and her husband, Craig's son, Craig Jr. and his girlfriend, Craig's daughter, Jennifer and her boyfriend. It was significant to begin meeting Craig's family. I felt welcome and accepted.

Later that evening Craig presented me with the engagement ring that he and Sherri had designed. It was beautiful with three marquee and four baguette diamonds. That weekend the ring was a big topic of conversation.

The next day the engagement party on the dock was lively and fun. The food was fantastic and Craig's friends were all warm and welcoming.

November Engagement Party in Marina del Rey

I had a long conversation with Craig's friend, Gil, in the cockpit of Craig's boat. I found Gil to be a very sincere person and I sensed that he wanted to get to know me because he obviously had high regard for Craig and loved him very much. Gil was looking out for Craig's best interest and this whirlwind romance was happening so quickly, everyone was questioning Craig's judgment. I got to know Gil that day and it helped me comprehend the high caliber of Craig's friends; they all seemed to have a heartfelt connection with Craig.

Though everyone was friendly and jovial, I was totally being checked out, but I felt like I had passed the test. Becoming part of Craig's group of family and friends felt fantastic. I had a wonderful time.

On my flight home, Craig surprised me with an upgraded seat in First Class.

Celebration

• *Mishael*

Every weekend had always been focused on fun activities. There was so much to see and do in the wine country, and I was always looking for new places to go and things to do. Now it was time to introduce Craig to my immediate family members. I was very excited about the Thanksgiving holiday. On Wednesday we were going to Sonora to my cousin Carol's cabin for a big family gathering. On Friday we were coming back to Calistoga to get ready for a family gathering at the cottage on Saturday.

As we were getting ready for the holiday, we realized that we were on the same wavelength both preferring neat, tidy and organized. Once again, Craig and I were in tune, not only with matching hiking boots, but we had similar desires regarding organized households and being prepared for guests. We realized we were a good team, not just for fun, but for getting necessary chores done too.

My son, Lance, was driving from Eugene, Oregon with my parents. Lots of family members would be present at Carol's cabin in Sonora and there was great anticipation and excitement about meeting Craig. At this point, we were a committed couple and I had an engagement ring on my finger.

Lance and my parents arrived in Calistoga on Wednesday and meeting Craig went well. Lance rode with me and Craig to Sonora, so the three of us were in the car together and we had fun chatting and laughing. Immediately, the two Aries guys teamed up together and established a pattern of playfully teasing me that continues to this day.

The cabin was beautiful and it was refreshing to be in the mountains. We had a traditional Thanksgiving dinner. Craig and I prepared a sautéed green bean dish to contribute to the meal. I was pleased observing Craig's spontaneity and comfort with my family.

We went to Jamestown, a state park and old gold mining town and we explored the area. Lance had fun seeing his cousins, Shawnie, Carrie and Dana. Carrie received news that she had passed the Bar that weekend. There was much to celebrate and we all had a great time.

Craig was his usual funny, charming and darling self and was immediately loved and adored by my family. Our relationship was moving quickly, but the fact that my family so wholeheartedly loved him was confirmation that I hadn't gone off the deep end. It was wonderful to have the blessing of my family.

• *Craig*

I was excited about this trip to the cabin in Sonora, as well as meeting Mishael's family. We took sleeping bags and assumed we would bunk, on the floor, with the young people.

Much to our surprise, we were shocked when Carol showed us where we would be sleeping. She had set up a bed for Mishael and me on the stairway landing. It seemed we were the center of attention that weekend, the entire family was watching us. I was extremely nervous, but I figured that since the bed was set up for us, with her father there, that I had been accepted by her family and that made my heart sing.

• *Mishael*

We drove back to Calistoga on Friday to get ready for the Saturday evening dinner party at the cottage. I was excited about hosting a party where more of my family would be present. Lance and my Mom and Dad would be there, along with my Aunt Barbara, my cousin Kevin and wife and daughter, and my cousin Leroy and his wife. I had also invited my biological brother, Michael, from the San Jose area, to join us.

Michael knew Lance but he had never met anyone else in my family. He had recently experienced a tragedy in his life. His 16-year old son had died in an automobile accident the day before his 17th birthday, which sent his wife, Cindy, into a total tailspin; their marriage was quietly dissolving. Michael was grieving the death of a child, divorce seemed inevitable and he needed someone to talk to. During that time, Michael and I had many long phone conversations, were supportive of each other and became very close.

In 1982, at age 32, I had met my biological parents, Verne and Reane McGlothlen, my older brother Michael, his wife and their son, my younger half-sister, Michelle and her husband, and their two sons. Now that I lived in Calistoga I was closer in proximity than ever before to my birth family. I really wanted Michael to meet Craig and was happy that he would also meet my parents and some of my immediate family as well.

I was delighted to show off my hostess skills. I prefer non-traditional so I prepared a fabulous vegetarian meal. I served several quiches with salads, all of the trimmings and delightful pear pie for dessert. Everything was prepared from scratch, and beautifully pre-sented, so lots of preparation went into getting ready. This was the first party Craig and I hosted together and he was impressed with my culinary and hostess skills.

We spent Christmas 1990 in Marina del Rey and I finally met Craig's mother, Gloria, for the first time. She was delightful, fun and funny, just like Craig. We spent Christmas Day with Gloria and Craig's sister Sherri and her husband. There was a light-hearted feeling of jovial fun and camaraderie in his family. The next day we drove south to Vista, California where I met Craig's brother Kirk, his wife and their darling children. I loved Craig's family and was excited about joining such a fun family. I had hit the jackpot!

• *Craig*

Christmas was special that year, because Mishael met my mother, my brother and more of my family. We had a really fun holiday. She flew down to Los Angeles and we drove back to Calistoga together.

When we arrived in Calistoga, much to our surprise, there had been a freeze and all of the pipes in her cottage had frozen and burst. Since the house had well water, and the water had frozen, the pump had burned out and this created a problem. It took a few days to get things thawed out and repaired. We managed to get through the mess and made the best of the weekend, the cozy fireplace came in handy.

• *Mishael*

Craig came to my office Christmas Party and Estela, one of the AWC gals, had a New Year's Eve Party that we attended along with all of the other AWC women. It seemed like my life had become one big celebration. In January we made a trip to Oregon to spend time with my parents and introduce Craig to my Oregon friends.

My friend, Susie Leo, hosted an Engagement Party for us in Eugene and all my friends showed up from years past. Kenda, my friend from Washington, drove down from Seattle and we were delighted to discover that Kenda and Craig shared an April 12th birthday. Everyone scrutinized Craig very closely. Craig was so charming and delightful that all of my friends immediately loved him. In my heart, I knew the relationship was very special, but to have that confirmation, from the people I loved most, was helpful and confirmed that committing to marriage, even after a very short courtship, was not absolutely crazy.

Connection

• *Mishael*

It was really fun the way our courtship began. A long distance relationship was the perfect way for me to ease into a partnership as I had quite an established solo routine. In the mornings, six days a week, I ran 5 miles. During the week I worked in a busy office. In the evenings, usually four to five times per week, I went to the local gym in downtown Calistoga. By choice, I hadn't had a television for ten years, I enjoyed listening to music, reading, journaling, cooking and being by myself in the evenings. But, I thoroughly looked forward to three and four-day weekends with Craig.

The anticipation of being together and sharing activities the next weekend was so exciting it was almost unbearable. Our time together was so wonderful and it seemed that everything we did was romantic.

Back in those days, not everyone had a personal computer and there was no such thing as email. During the week, even though we talked frequently by phone, we had a strong desire for connection; so we sent cards. I found writing helpful to sort out the barrage of thoughts and feelings swirling inside me.

• *Craig*

Receiving cards from Mishael was incredibly exciting; it really helped cement our love connection. It was fun for me to express, in writing, what I was feeling. This was something I had never done before. I went to the Hallmark store and dove into the cards; I loved choosing cards for her. Writing and receiving cards helped bring us closer together, because even though we couldn't always see each other, we expressed written heart-felt feelings.

• *Mishael*

I had quite a supply of cards; I was sending one and sometimes two cards a day when Craig was in Marina del Rey. Frequently, when we wandered through the boutiques, shops and bookstores in Calistoga, we would sneak and buy cards for each other that we would send in the following weeks. Even in those early days it was all about finding ways to create surprise and delight.

Chapter Four
Wedding Bells

"You are the sunshine of my life,
that's why I'll always be around.
You are the apple of my eye.
Forever you'll stay in my heart."
--Stevie Wonder

Moving From the Cottage

• Craig

When it was time to go home, I hated saying goodbye, and I missed her when we were apart. My heart felt at home when I was with Mishael.

After the weekend of frozen pipes in Calistoga, driving home was sad and lonely, but it gave me time to contemplate the future and I realized how much I loved her.

We had discussed ending our long distance commute and living together. I even considered transferring to San Francisco. We loved the city but decided the weather there was too cold. We preferred the idea of Mishael moving to live with me. With the recent freeze in Calistoga, it seemed that sooner would be better than later to make the move.

• Mishael

As we were planning our future together we needed to decide what to do. Craig could easily transfer to San Francisco, but the cold weather in San Francisco did not appeal to us. My position as a Legal Records Manager, in a law firm, wasn't worth writing home about, so I was willing to take on the challenge of uprooting myself, going to a new area, securing employment and creating an entirely new life.

Craig did all of the legwork of finding an apartment in his area. We continued to have fun on the weekends as we worked out the details of our plans to live together. This was a very exciting time for us.

• *Craig*

Obviously, there wasn't room for all of Mishael's shoes on the boat. The Moonshadow was small for one person to live aboard, I folded my t-shirts like burritos to fit in the drawers.

After living on the boat for seven years, moving on land was a thrilling transition for me. I had found a cute apartment to move into so we could set up house.

We loaded up Raja and the contents of the cottage and drove to El Segundo on Valentine's Day 1991 to begin our future together. We had so much fun on the drive talking, laughing and planning; we were so excited about our future that we kept pinching each other and asking if this was really happening. We didn't know why our love was so strong but we were very optimistic and happy.

• *Mishael*

On the drive south, Raja was in a kitty carrier. He howled and sang cat songs for the entire trip. When we arrived in El Segundo, it became apparent that Raja would have to become an indoor cat; outside would not be a safe option for him in such an urban location. It made me sad to think that Raja's days in the orchard and vineyards were over. We began to discuss the possibility of a better life for Raja.

Craig worked with a delightful man at Delta, Julian, who was willing to take Raja into his household of children and pets. Raja fit right in and the doll house in the backyard patio soon became Raja's house. It was a sad day when Raja left me and Craig but I knew life in an apartment would not be good for him. Raja became fat and lazy and lived happily ever after with Julian's family.

Getting Married

• *Mishael*

We set the wedding date for August 10th, which gave us several months to prepare and get ready. We chose Barnaby's, a marvelous boutique hotel on Sepulveda Boulevard in Manhattan Beach, which was filled with antique furniture and Old World art. Barnaby's no longer exists, it has been remodeled and modernized; today it is called The Belamar Hotel.

We met with David, Sherri's jeweler friend, and designed a wedding band, with baguette diamonds, to go with the engagement ring. Later I met with David and chose a beautiful wedding ring for Craig and presented it as a surprise.

Friday, August 9, 1991

• *Craig*

Barnaby's had a beautiful garden area with a bougainvillea-covered gazebo, where we were going to have the ceremony. It was nice that my family could arrive and stay in the same hotel where the wedding was and convenient for people from out of town. At the wedding rehearsal, the day before the wedding, I saw many friends and family arriving. Everyone delighted in our happiness and was thrilled about our wedding.

I was so happy to have my son and daughter in the wedding party. I wanted them to understand how much I loved Mishael and to see what a special relationship and bond we had. I hoped that by seeing our true love that one day they would experience it themselves.

Once again, celebration summed up what we were up to. We had a lovely rehearsal dinner at Reuben's, one of my Happy Hour haunts in Marina del Rey; I knew the staff and they were happy for us. From our huge table that seated twenty, we could look out and see the marina. Our mothers, our children, my brother and sister, Sherri, Mishael's friend, Karen, and all of their significant others were in attendance. This was the first time our families had come together. Mishael's father was 79 years old and, though he supported our marriage, he chose not to make the trip to southern California for the wedding.

That night we had fun with our guests. I had the most fun making eyes at my honey; it was so much fun to hug and kiss her in front of everybody.

After the rehearsal dinner, it was late and Lance and I stayed at our apartment...no bachelor party for me. I wanted to be bright-eyed and on time for our date with the Minister.

I was excited about marrying Mishael because I truly felt I had found a part of me that was missing for so many years; I knew I had found my soul mate. It was so wonderful to have somebody in my life with whom I could demonstrate my love and affection. I received the same love from her and that's what made our relationship so strong. In a way, I felt as though Mishael and I were finishing something that started long ago and now we were completing our life as one.

• *Mishael*

I met Craig shortly after my 40th birthday and here we were getting married the weekend after my 41st birthday. Though it would have been easy to say, "No, let's not take a chance," Craig and

I realized that we had something special together and needed to move forward. Of course there was risk and no guarantee of a happy future. Here I was starting over, I had uprooted myself, moved to a new area and was living with someone I had known for only eleven months. I had secured employment as a Business Office Manager at a heart institute in Santa Monica. Everything seemed to be falling into place and when I make a commitment, I give my all.

In some way, it felt like Craig and I were twins. We seemed to be on the same wavelength about so many things. We thought the same way, we observed things the same way and it felt right to be a committed team. And now, we would soon be sealing the deal with a wedding.

After the rehearsal dinner, my Mom and I shared a room at Barnaby's and spent the late evening hanging out with family in the hotel.

Saturday, August 10, 1991

• *Craig*

It turned out to be a beautiful day; the hotel staff said it was the only day in August that the sun came out. Getting ready was a lot of fun, I was getting dressed in a room with Craig Jr. and Lance. For the boys it was a good time for bonding. I was extremely excited and the boys tried to calm me down. Once I was dressed, I was meeting and greeting guests as they arrived. Craig Jr. and Lance seated the guests.

My daughter, Jennifer, arrived with her six-month old baby, Kevin, in a car seat. When she went to get dressed, I took the baby and went out to where everyone was seated and said, "Look, we've already got a baby!" That got everybody laughing.

The Minister looked at me and said, "Craig, you need some calming down. Come with me." He took me into the bar and asked the bartender to give me something strong and straight. The bartender handed me a shot of Jack Daniels and the Minister said, "Drink it, don't sip it. I want you to drink this whole thing down." So I did and we laughed. I couldn't wait for the ceremony to begin.

• *Mishael*

Our wedding party consisted of Craig's children, Craig Jr. and Jennifer, my son, Lance, and my friend, Karen, from Bend, Oregon. When my mother walked me down the aisle and I looked out into the crowd, I wondered, "Who are all these people at my wedding?" There were a lot of Craig's cousins I hadn't met yet and many people that he worked with; they were all new faces and it was shocking to see so many people I didn't know at my wedding. Kristen was there from the AWC.

Saying our vows and exchanging rings

Wedding party. Jennifer, Karen, Mishael, Craig, Craig Jr. and Lance

Craig looked so handsome that day. It felt wonderful to suddenly be part of such a large family and group of friends.

A great party on our special day

We had a lovely reception and enjoyed dancing in the hotel later that evening. We were in the honeymoon suite, with all of the trimmings, including chocolate dipped strawberries and champagne. Somewhere in the back of our closets, we still have our robes from Barnaby's.

Honeymoon in Mammoth

• *Craig*

Mishael and I couldn't wait to go on our honeymoon. We took our new honeymoon car that we had purchased in July. Our dear friends, Gil and Louise, offered us their condo in Mammoth, California. We loved the mountains, outdoor activities and the opportunity to unwind and be in nature was very desirable. Thank you, Gil and Louise!

Now we were married!! This was a wonderful time for us to bond and be alone as we began our married life together. With the stresses of work and planning a wedding behind us, we had time to reflect on where we had been and where we were going. I felt complete in every way, physically, emotionally and mentally. The future was ahead of us and we knew we were an awesome couple.

• *Mishael*

Our first night in Mammoth we went out to dinner at Shogun, a Japanese restaurant. After dinner we played backgammon in the lounge and Craig won every game. I thought I was a backgammon pro, but he showed me a thing or two.

Our honeymoon was wonderful. The hiking there was incredible, the views were spectacular and we truly enjoyed being in nature.

Hiking in Mammoth was fantastic

The views on our hikes were breathtaking

Every day we planned a new hiking adventure. We hiked on the John Muir Trail, went to Devil's Postpile and Rainbow Falls, and we took a tram to the summit of Mammoth Mountain at 11,000 feet. We also went to Bodi, an old mining town and to Mono Lake, an ancient lake with "tufa", incredible formations in and around the lake. To us it was all romantic and adventurous.

The best part was that it was a new beginning for us. In eleven months we had made a big commitment, and we were beginning our married life together. We said our vows in the presence of our family and friends and we were beginning a wonderful new life. I felt secure and complete; I was entering this new chapter in my life with a solid companion. I knew we were a dynamic team and together would make a significant contribution.

Chapter Five
One Year Later

"Love doesn't make the world go 'round.
Love is what makes the ride worthwhile."
--Franklin P. Jones

• Mishael

As I look back and reflect on how I was feeling in the summer of
1992; I was intoxicated with the joyful feeling of being in love and
on an incredible adventure with my husband. By this time, two years
into the relationship and one year into the marriage, I had quit giving
myself a hard time about blindly rushing into a relationship. Now
our marriage had a solid, established foundation; we were happy,
our marriage was filled with love and laughter and our relationship
seemed to be getting better and better. At the end of each day,
when I knew I would see Craig, I had that excited feeling of anticipation. It still felt like those earlier days when I was driving to the Pink
Flamingo Hotel to meet Craig. I am happy to say that, to this day,
I still experience that exhilarating feeling of excitement when I am
going to see Craig, especially when the weekend is near and I am
anticipating our Friday night date or a weekend of fun activities.

Anniversary Holiday

• Mishael

In August 1992 we went to the British Virgin Islands (BVI) on a
bareboat charter with our good friends, and excellent travel compan-
ions, Gil and Louise. The goal of this trip was to celebrate our first
wedding anniversary. The BVI is an exotic tropical heaven, a sailor's

paradise with the trade winds always blowing. Though we went to many islands, we didn't have to pack and catch trains and planes; our boat took us to each new destination. It was a very relaxing, romantic and magical holiday.

Our first stop, after leaving the mainland, was in San Juan, Puerto Rico where we had incredibly luxurious accommodations. The plane ride from San Juan to Tortola was a frightening adventure with a very casual pilot, on what appeared to be a poorly maintained airplane, but we made it. Upon arrival, at Nanny Cay, we were upgraded to a 42 foot Catalina instead of the 38 foot Beneteau that we had reserved. The boat was packed with food we had ordered to meet our eating preferences.

Each night in the cockpit we would look at maps and determine our destination for the next day. Most islands we went to were not highly populated. Norman Island had nothing on it; we ate and drank at William Thornton Bar and Restaurant on an old pirate ship anchored in a cove called the Bight. This is the island and cove about which Robert Louis Stevenson wrote *Treasure Island* and it was near Treasure Point, where it is said pirates hid their treasure, that I had my first snorkeling experience.

The trade winds are always blowing in Sir Francis Drake Channel, a sailor's paradise

On Peter Island there was nothing but a restaurant and a dive shop. On Beef Island, we went to a place called DeLoose Mongoose Beach Club, the rum drinks called No See Em's were superbly intoxicating. Virgin Gorda is a geological phenomenon and wonderland of giant granite boulders where the snorkeling was out of this world. We exchanged yacht club flags at the Bitter End Yacht Club. In Cane Garden Harbor we were serenaded to sleep by reggae music from a restaurant on the beach. Sandy Cay was totally uninhabited and like a picture perfect postcard. On Yost Van Dyke at Foxy's, we sat with our feet in the sand and enjoyed funny political songs sang by a man with a guitar who took time out from working on his boat to entertain us.

• *Craig*

August 10th, the day of our wedding anniversary, we were docked in Road Harbour, Tortola. Gil and Louise presented us with a bottle of champagne for a toast and a beautifully framed photo that they had taken of us a few weeks earlier when we were together at the Pageant of the Masters in Laguna Beach, California.

August 10, 1992, first wedding anniversary in Road Harbour, Tortola, BVI

That evening we went to Pusser's Outpost, a nautical museum, retail shop and restaurant, so named for Pusser's Rum that the British Royal Navy provided for their sailors. It was a delightful evening of exquisite dining and lots of laughter.

Dinner at Pusser's Outpost with Gil and Louise

Returning to Nanny Cay the winds were strong, the main sail blew out and we were chased out of the islands by Hurricane Andrew. It never dampened our spirits and we have continued our honeymoon to this day.

• *Mishael*

On the return trip while we were waiting for our flight to San Juan, we were in a cafeteria at the airport in Tortola, where there were trays that could be slid along a counter to the cashier. We all noticed a woman with a cane enter the cafeteria. As everyone in the room looked up and noticed her we were all thinking, *How is she going to manage a tray with her cane?* It seemed as if everything and everyone was in slow motion, except for Craig. As everyone watched, Craig immediately jumped up to assist the woman with her tray and he graciously helped her to a table. It seemed Craig was the only one that immediately recognized and acted on the right thing to do.

This is an example of how Craig goes through life, without hesitation he always sees what needs to be done and does it right away. He is exceptionally helpful and generous with his time. I am extremely proud to be his wife.

Chapter Six
Through the Years

"Trouble is part of life and if you don't share it,
you don't give the person who loves you
a chance to love you enough."
--Dinah Shore

Though we have had a stellar relationship and many magical moments, we have not had a Pollyanna-type life. We have had some of the same problems and challenges that all families experience. Locking arms and facing challenges together, with a "we'll get through this together" attitude, has been an approach that has worked for us. Being a team has given us courage and our love has given us strength and carried us through difficult periods.

1990 – Challenges of Joining a Family

• Mishael

Craig's two children, Craig Jr. and Jennifer, had always been the center of Craig's Universe. In September 1990, when Craig and I met; Jennifer was 18, had just graduated from high school and was pregnant with a baby due in January 1991. Even though Jennifer had lots of girlfriends, a boyfriend, and many social activities, she thoroughly enjoyed the attention of her father because it is delightful to be the focus of Craig's attention. Jennifer knew her mother wasn't the love of her Dad's life but she kind of felt like perhaps she was. It was somewhat disconcerting for Jennifer when I came on the scene. Suddenly Craig had a busy life; was often out of town on weekends, had activities planned, and frequently wasn't available without advance notice.

Once, when quite a few people were on the dock with us for a barbecue, Craig said, "Honey, will you please bring me the lemon pepper from the galley?"

I quickly responded, "Yes, I'll get it."

In dismay, Jennifer said to her Dad, "I used to be your Honey!"

It is always difficult for children, when their dad has a new bride and it was evident that there were some issues at hand.

Through the years I have always encouraged a close father-daughter relationship, created time for Craig and Jennifer to be together without me and I have always been very kind and supportive of Jennifer's three children. After many years Craig's happiness has continued to be radiant and I have earned my place in the family.

Gloria, Craig's Mother, had a difficult time accepting that Craig was head-over-heels in a love relationship. We were committed and engaged before I met any of Craig's family. Gloria was anxious and worried that the relationship was moving too quickly, and rightly so. There was a time when Craig took his mother out for evenings of dinner and dancing. They always teased, laughed and had a great time. Gloria feared that her relationship with Craig, her "touchstone", was forever changing.

Over time Gloria realized that Craig's relationship with me was uniquely special, that Craig continued to be over-joyed with love and she was always supportive of our relationship. Craig and Gloria talked frequently and continued to have a very close relationship.

Even in the most supportive and loving families, it is challenging to enter a family as a new bride and be immediately accepted by everyone. The Patton family had a long history that did not include me and that I could never be part of. To some degree, I will always be an outsider, always new to the clan even though I have accumulated two decades of history with them. I've made my way and carved out a place for myself in the family by being kind and thoughtful. I continue to encourage Craig to have time with his family when I am not present. It is very special when you can have Craig all to yourself and I want all of them to continue to have that opportunity.

• *Craig*

When I met Mishael I never imagined that I could fall in love so quickly. I wasn't sure what was happening but I was excited to tell everyone I had met someone I thought I could truly be happy with for the rest of my life even though I hadn't known her very long. In our early courtship, I was commuting to Napa Valley and spending three and four-day weekends with Mishael. It was hard for my family to understand that I wouldn't always be available for them at a moment's notice. My love for them hadn't changed, but I had intimate love brewing that was moving me in a new direction.

Living on the boat was convenient for my Mom. When she called and needed help with something, I could be at her house in fifteen minutes. And the same was true for my daughter, Jennifer. I was still available for them when they needed me, but not always immediately. The fact that I wasn't there as often for my Mom and daughter had a big impact on them, even though my love for them never changed. Craig Jr. reacted somewhat differently than Jennifer and my Mother; he understood that I was overjoyed and realized how long I had been lonesome for companionship.

2002 and 2009 – Death of Family

• *Mishael*

Death of a parent is always difficult. My Dad was the lighthouse of my life; he loved me without condition which was a very important life-lesson. My father had bladder cancer and because of heart problems, surgery to remove the cancer could not be completed.

In January 2001 the doctor told me that my dad was very old, had bladder cancer, severe heart problems, and that one of those three things would eventually take his life. Fortunately, I had one year to mentally prepare and begin grieving before my Dad passed. Because my Dad was so significant in my life, I feared that when he passed I would not be able to function as a wife or in life. I worried that my relationship with Craig would not survive the death of my Dad when he passed away in February 2002. I was amazed that the sun came up the next day and the world kept spinning; the world seemed oblivious that such a significant person had left the planet.

Craig seemed to have an innate sense that I needed to grieve in my own way and on my own time. Craig gave me a lot of space to do what I needed to do to survive the death of my Dad; he was very loving and supportive throughout my grieving process. Because of Craig's unconditional love, I survived the death of my Dad and was able to function.

In 2009 when Craig's mother passed away I was extremely worried about Craig and his sister, Sherri. They were both so close to their mother; I knew they were devastated. I wanted to be there for them in every way but at the same time I wanted to give them space to grieve in a way that was right for them. It is a very difficult family situation to be in when you want to help but there is nothing you can do.

• *Craig*

When Mishael's father's health began to deteriorate I could see that she was hurting inside. It was difficult for her to express her feelings so I encouraged Mishael to be more open and share her thoughts. In the last year of his life there were many times when Mishael's Dad had close calls, but somehow he always managed to pull through. In February 2002 when we got the call from Mishael's Mother, the Hospice Nurse had said his body was beginning to shut down so I encouraged Mishael to fly out the next day and I am glad she took my advice. We got the call on Monday evening, Mishael arrived on Tuesday afternoon, and her Dad passed away on Thursday morning with Mishael and her Mother at his bedside. Many times I have heard Mishael say that she's so glad she was with her Dad at the time of his death; she considers it a beautiful passing.

In July 2009 when my Mother passed away I was grateful that I was with her and glad that I had the love and support of Mishael and my family and friends to help me get through the grief. Being supported by ones that you love makes all the difference in challenging times.

2004 – Financial Difficulties

• *Mishael*

When Craig and I got together we were accustomed to managing our finances independently. Initially Craig took care of the expenses for the boat and I took care of the household expenses. We both contributed to groceries, gas, and various other expenses. Later, in 1995 when we sold the boat, we divided the household expenses but there was no reason to co-mingle our income. We didn't even have a joint checking account until 2002, 11 years into our marriage when we sold a home and needed a joint account for the sale proceeds.

In 2003 I started an at-home business, spent a lot of money on advertising and accumulated significant debt. I was disappointed with my lack of success and kept thinking that if I continued, I would be able to turn it around and eliminate the debt. I did not want to disappoint Craig and as time passed, I found it extremely difficult to communicate to Craig about the severity of our financial situation. Keeping financial secrets brought misery and emotional stress that was unbearable. Finally, I had to tell Craig about the debt, he was shocked and disappointed that I hadn't confided in him. We became stronger and sturdier as we joined together to tackle this problem and recover from the debt. Now we both participate in all financial decisions. Craig's ongoing love and encouragement has never wavered; our love has sustained us through challenging financial difficulties.

• *Craig*

Our financial status was stable for many years as we enjoyed two full incomes. In 1999 when I retired from Delta Airlines; it had a substantial negative impact on our income so I secured other employment and our finances stabilized. Mishael's employer went out of business and she tried working from home, which I thought it was a great idea. However, she incurred substantial debt which I was initially not aware of. Mishael brooded about this problem and finally opened up to me. I wasn't as upset about the debt as I was about Mishael being afraid to tell me. It was a tough time, but through working together and being honest with each other; we worked it out and have recovered. This incident contributed to a big lesson for us about open and honest communication.

<u>2005 – Accident and Injury</u>

• *Mishael*

In August of 2005 I attended a seminar in Irvine, California. On the second day of the seminar I fell down some stairs and was taken to the hospital with a dislocated left fibula, fractured left tibia, and a right foot bone chip. I had surgery and a six inch titanium rod, one pin and eight screws were installed into my left ankle. The next day I had to demonstrate that I could walk with crutches, on my fractured right foot, before they would release me from the hospital.

Craig was a true champion. He immediately assumed all household duties, including grocery shopping and meal preparation. Initially I needed help washing my hair. Do you remember the scene in *Out of Africa* when Robert Redford washed Meryl Streep's hair? Aside from being on crutches and miserable in every way, Craig washing my hair was romantic and wonderful. Soon I got a bath bench and could wash my hair in the shower. However, bathing and getting dressed was a two-hour time consuming challenge and I needed help getting in and out of the shower, so I did all of my personal care at night when Craig was available to assist me.

I continued to work five days a week, but came home so exhausted that often all I could do was fall into bed and cry. Recovery seemed like such a long and difficult uphill path. After the cast came off Craig changed the dressing every day. I was on crutches for over three months, had to learn to walk, had six months of difficult physical therapy with lots of at-home exercises and had a terrible limp for eight long months.

Craig was a superb caregiver; he assisted me with all of my physical and tremendous emotional needs. Once again, it was love that sustained us.

• *Craig*

When Mishael was out of town at a seminar, she had an accident and had surgery. I felt really bad for her but it gave me an opportunity to show Mishael how much I loved her. I did everything possible to ease her situation, it was quite a task. I had to be strong and I encouraged Mishael to be even stronger. As a team, I knew we would get through it together.

<u>Summary</u>

Even though our hardships may seem small compared to what other families go through, these have been some of our challenges. Tremendous love, care, honesty, support and respect have carried us through our adversities. For us, love has been the key to meeting our challenges and has contributed to our happiness and relationship success.

Chapter Seven
How We Thrive

"The life and love we create is the life and love we live."
--Leo Buscaglia

Being on the same wavelength in so many areas of our life has been paramount to our relationship success.

Health and Wellness

• *Mishael*

Beginning in the mid-seventies, I began moving in the direction of healthy foods. I became committed to optimum health and wellness which entails meal planning, shopping, meal preparation and taking food with me when I am away from home. I choose restaurants that offer healthy choices; fast food is never an acceptable option.

I enjoy preparing food with a loving attitude and presenting it beautifully. I believe the spirit and attitude of love contributes to overall good health. Craig is happy to eat such fine food; he brags, carries on about my cooking and is my biggest fan. Most importantly, Craig is willing to participate in my health and wellness techniques and philosophy. I am also working on a book about optimum health and wellness with a companion cookbook.

We are committed to an active lifestyle that includes exercise. We anticipate being healthy, well and active together into old age because we take very good care of ourselves.

• *Craig*

Before I met Mishael I was moving in the direction of healthier food; I had eliminated red meat and ate very little chicken. Mishael introduced me to a simple, near-vegetarian, healthy eating-style that I found delicious. She has wooed my family and our friends with healthy gourmet meals. We enjoy entertaining and feeding people food that contributes to good health. I have learned so much from Mishael about cooking that I am working on a cook-book, with healthy, quick and easy recipes for busy families.

<u>Lifestyle</u>

• *Mishael*

I delight in the couple-ness Craig and I have created. We seem to see things in the same way, make similar observations, and often speak at the same time with parallel thoughts. I treasure our relationship and take good care of it. Being in a committed relationship, and part of a powerful team, is a fabulous way to go through life.

• *Craig*

After my first marriage ended my main focus was always my children and my family. I enjoyed the marina community and I looked out for everyone and always knew what was happening on our dock. I have always been very social, out-going and the life-of-the-party kind of guy; but after everyone went home I was alone and lonely.

When I met Mishael the pledge I had made, at the end of my first marriage, about not wanting to get married again, quickly dissolved. I wanted a very nice wedding so our children could participate in the ceremony and celebrate our coming together with our friends and extended families.

Level of Happiness

• *Mishael*

In some ways, my early life was like walking down a narrow, poorly-lit corridor. When I met Craig, my happiness level went from a 3 to 15, on a scale of 1-10. It was like I was suddenly joyfully dancing and twirling in bright sunlight.

And now with my career as an Author and Speaker, I am living my life purpose, contributing, making a difference and feeling tremendously fulfilled.

• *Craig*

Meeting Mishael has certainly raised the level of happiness in my life. Our long distance relationship added a lot of anticipation, excitement and adventure to our early courtship. My happiness continues to grow and evolve each year. I realize that our marriage is exceptional because I don't see or know couples that share the level of companionship and extreme love and care that we celebrate.

Attitude

• *Mishael*

An attitude of gratitude is truly where it's at. Often we have a tendency to take things for granted when we have so many things to be thankful for. Craig and I have health and wellness, our children and extended families are well, we are in love and we live in a wonderful home in the desert in which we love to share time with family and friends. I am joyful for the simple pleasures that we experience every day. If we were to make a list of all of the good things going on in our life; the list would be very long. I feel blessed and every day I am grateful for my relationship with Craig.

• *Craig*

When I met Mishael I had a bitter and angry attitude toward women and relationships. I now understand that my negative attitude was detrimental to my post-marriage relationships. I quickly realized that Mishael was genuine and a loving and caring person; I felt she was someone I could spend my life with. My attitude quickly improved and continues to be positive and happy every day.

<u>Playfulness and Fun</u>

• *Mishael*

I grew up in a family that was very serious. Nobody really knew how to be playful and have fun. We were careful not to hurt each other's feelings and the cards we exchanged were always very serious. By contrast, Craig is vivacious, fun and funny and his family exchanges very funny cards. Craig is willing to be silly and foolish and he is happiest when he makes everyone laugh. He often teases and sometimes mimics me in a playful and loving way.

Living with Craig is so much fun; we often laugh and get hysterically carried away. Sometimes I worry that we are going to disturb the entire neighborhood. With Craig's help I have learned to have fun and be funny. I have become quick to laugh, and now enjoy being silly and having fun. My evolution into becoming a fun and funny person is an on-going process that gives me great pleasure. I choose never to regress to a life of seriousness. A life without laughter is truly not worth living.

• *Craig*

Growing up I had very close relationships with my brother, sisters, and cousins. Being silly and having fun was the way we interacted. As an adult, I have continued to tease and play and I totally enjoy making people laugh. I love to be foolish, lighten the mood, and bring smiles to people's faces.

A big component of my relationship with Mishael is humor; we love to laugh and have fun, even in difficult times. I have thoroughly enjoyed helping Mishael see the happy and fun side of life.

Life Purpose

• *Mishael*

My purpose is to be loving and help people heal their hearts with love. I have come to a place in my life where everything is about love. I am so fortunate to be with my perfect companion and participate every day in a loving relationship. We have created our company, Love Heals Hearts, to promote our books, movies, products and services to heal the planet and radiate love throughout the Universe.

• *Craig*

My life purpose is to be kind, helpful and generous. I thoroughly enjoy identifying needs, helping people and spreading joy and laughter. I also enjoy talking about Mishael and our extreme level of happiness. By sharing our how-we-met love story; we hope that we are giving people inspiration and an opportunity to see that middle-aged people can meet, love each other deeply and live happily ever-after. We are a perfect example of a relationship that has evolved and gotten better and better year after year.

Chapter Eight
Ways to Show Love

"I want to kiss you all over,
and over again,
'til the night rushes in."
--Mike Chapman and Nicky Chinn

The Magic of Love Strategies™

How do you show love? How do you demonstrate that you love your partner? How does your partner know that you love them?

Love strategies™ are gestures of love and can be very simple, very extravagant, or anywhere in between. The goal is to please and pleasure your partner. The more love strategies, the better the relationship. Contributing to make the household run smoothly also counts; having an organized and well-run household contributes to everyone's happiness and is an important love strategy.

We have each listed some things that we do to demonstrate our love. Following that is a list of things that we both do. Look them over and decide which ones you are going to try.

Love Strategies™

• *Mishael*

- Does most of the grocery shopping and laundry;
- Prepares and presents meals, with a loving attitude, at the "Love Table" or at the "Patton's Café" in our back patio;
- Makes every meal a celebration, beautifully presented, often with candles;

- Prepares healthy food and promotes optimum health and wellness;
- Created pet names for Craig: "Honeydoll", "Precious" and "Precious One";
- Strongly supports and brags about Craig's commitment to Search and Rescue (DSSAR) volunteer activities;
- Prepares "Hero Dinners" when Craig returns from DSSAR activities;
- Is always kind and supportive; and
- Turns down the bed and arranges pillows.

• *Craig*

- Always has complements for Mishael;
- Is proud of Mishael and brags about everything she does;
- Adores Mishael's body, just the way it is;
- Teases in a playful and fun way;
- Promotes laughter and hilarity;
- Often cleans up the kitchen after dinner;
- Encourages and emotionally supports Mishael in every imaginable way;
- Washes and takes care of all maintenance for Mishael's car;
- Does laundry; and
- Does EVERYTHING around the house, inside and outside.

• *Mishael and Craig*

- Say "I love you" dozens of times each day;
- Demonstrate love in very silly ways;
- Are playful, have fun, and laugh together every day;
- Are kind and considerate;
- Frequently hold hands;
- Hide love notes for each other;
- Work together as a team to keep the household running smoothly, "Team House";
- Look for every opportunity to do something kind, helpful or thoughtful for each other;
- Support and encourage independent activities that they both enjoy;
- Celebrate the week with Friday night dates;
- Kiss at every arrival;
- Kiss at every departure;
- Kiss before each meal;
- Kiss before sleep;
- Cuddle and spoon in bed, "Calistoga Cuddle" (Mishael lays her head on Craig's left shoulder and drapes her legs around him);
- Enjoy full body, scented oil massages;
- Wash each other in the shower;
- Celebrate the day we met, September 13, 1990;
- Celebrate the day we moved to live together, February 14, 1991; and
- Celebrate our wedding anniversary, August 10, 1991.

<u>Love Notes</u>

• *Mishael*

One day, when I opened my lunchbox, I found a napkin on which Craig had written, with a yellow highlighter, "I love you". I was delighted to find such a sweet surprise. In the weeks that followed, I found another napkin in my lunchbox that said, "Way Much", because we often said, "I love you, way much". Later there was a third note on a piece of paper in a plastic baggie that said, "Love You". I began hiding those same notes for Craig, in all kinds of places: in a shoe, a shirt pocket, bathroom cabinet, jewelry box, coffee container, refrigerator or in his car.

Ten years later, we're still hiding those same three love notes for each other. Each time I find a note, it brings a smile to my face and I immediately hide the note for Craig to find. After ten years of playing this love note game, the challenge is to find new places to hide the notes. This is a very simple love strategy™ that creates surprise and delight and continues to be a lot of fun for us.

EXERCISE
WAYS TO SHOW LOVE

♥ How do you show love in your relationship? Make a
list of your current Love Strategies™.

_____

_____

_____

_____

_____

_____

_____

_____

_____

_____

_____

_____

_____

_____

_____

_____

_____

_____

_____

_____

EXERCISE
<u>WAYS TO DELIGHT YOUR PARTNER</u>

♥ Spend a few minutes and list some simple ways you
  can demonstrate your love and delight your partner.

_____

_____

_____

_____

_____

_____

_____

_____

_____

_____

_____

_____

_____

_____

_____

_____

_____

_____

_____

_____

_____

_____

♥ Review our Love Strategies™ and note which strategies you would like to model and incorporate into your relationship.

_____

_____

_____

_____

_____

_____

_____

_____

_____

_____

_____

_____

_____

_____

_____

_____

_____

_____

_____

_____

_____

_____

_____

_____

_____

101 Words That Describe Our Relationship

Here is a list of 101 words that describe our relationship:

Abundant

Adventurous

Affectionate

Amorous

Awesome

Balanced

Beautiful

Blissful

Brilliant

Captivating

Caring

Charming

Comfortable

Companionable

Compatible

Compassionate

Constructive

Co-operative

Creative

Delightful

Dynamic

Elegant

Enchanting

Endearing

Enduring

Energetic

Engaging

Enthusiastic

Enviable

Excellent

Exceptional

Exciting

Exhilarating

Fantastic

Fascinating

Friendly

Fulfilling

Fun

Funny

Generous

Glorious

Graceful

Happy

Healthy

Honest

Illuminating

Impressive

Incomprehensible

Incredible

Intense

Intimate

Inspirational

Joyful

Kind

Lively

Loving

Luminous

Luscious

Lustful

Hilarious

Magical

Magnetic

Magnanimous

Magnificent

Marvelous

Meaningful

Mirthful

Nurturing

Optimum

Outstanding

Passionate

Peaceful

Perceptive

Piquant

Playful

Pleasant

Pleasurable

Positive

Powerful

Precious

Profound

Relaxing

Responsive

Romantic

Sparkling

Sensual

Sharing

Sincere

Solid

Special

Spicy

Splendid

Stellar

Strong

Supportive

Teasing

Tremendous

Unselfish

Valuable

Vibrant

Zany

Do any of these words surprise you? Would you use any of these same words to describe your relationship? Very carefully choose the words you use to describe your relationship. You do have a choice. Know that the words you allow yourself to think, speak and describe your relationship will manifest as an element of your relationship.

EXERCISE
WORDS THAT DESCRIBE YOUR RELATIONSHIP

♥ Be creative, develop a list of words that describe the positive elements of your relationship.

_____

_____

_____

_____

_____

_____

_____

_____

_____

_____

_____

_____

_____

_____

_____

_____

_____

_____

_____

_____

_____

_____

_____

_____

Chapter Nine
Communication

"A kiss is a lovely trick, designed by nature,
to stop words when speech becomes superfluous."
--Ingrid Bergman

• *Mishael*

In the past I have often had a difficult time sorting out my thoughts to determine what I am thinking and how I am feeling. If a feeling of discomfort persists, I make it a priority to spend some time with myself to find out what is bothering me. I have found that journal writing is a helpful tool to get thoughts out of my head and onto paper, so I can better understand what is going on inside me.

On occasion, I have assumed that people can read my thoughts and know what I am thinking. Sometimes I have become so caught up in my perception and the story I have told myself about something that happened that I think others must know how I am feeling and what I am thinking. That is a very silly assumption that is never, ever going to happen.

I have learned that my perception is only my perception, based on my past experiences, and no one else is ever going to perceive anything exactly the way I do.

Communication is a key component in every successful relationship. It takes courage to say what I am thinking. When I communicate in the spirit of gentle kindness and love, Craig and I have always been very successful at resolving issues.

Communication Habits

I observed that my communication with my adopted-mother, Bonnie, was never honest. I carefully edited what I said, withheld information and felt that I always had to be careful not to upset her or hurt her feelings, because she might then reject me, like my birth-mother did. This was a story that I made up, as a little girl, and continued to live by, even as a mature adult. Many years later, I have discovered that my adopted-mother also edited information and was careful about what she said to me, because she also feared she might hurt my feelings and I would then reject her. We carefully tip-toed around each other; this is a very sad way to live, I don't recommend it.

My Mother and I have healed our relationship and now we make a conscious effort to be more bold and honest in our communication with each other and we have found that complete honesty has helped our relationship tremendously. Though we often catch ourselves slipping back into our old habit patterns, we have given each other permission to gently remind each other about our agreement to be completely honest.

I have observed that the way I communicated with my mother in the past for so many years, spilled over into the way I communicated with everyone in my life, including Craig. Though I consider myself to be very honest and have high integrity, often it takes a conscious effort to be bold, straight-forward and completely honest in all of my communication. Each time I risk and am completely honest, it works in my favor. But, I continue to work at it every day.

This old childhood communication style found its way into my communication with Craig; old habits die hard. Even though Craig loves me without condition, and would never reject me, sometimes I still catch myself editing and not telling the whole story, and for no reason, other than the comfort of an old habit pattern and communication style.

By contrast, every day Craig says funny, silly things and risks being rejected all of the time. I am currently enrolled in "Craig Patton's Be Silly School", I am signed up for Risk 101 and am making tremendous progress.

Take at look at your childhood communication style and determine if some of your old patterns persist. If your communication style is beneficial and positively contributes to your relationships, then continue on. However, if there is room for improvement, make a conscious effort to improve your communication skills. True and honest communication takes courage.

Communication System We Developed

Honesty is always the best policy. Withholding information from your partner, no matter how large or small, is never beneficial. When Craig and I have an issue or challenge, we call a family conference, put the issue on the table, examine it thoroughly and come up with possible solutions. Then we choose the best solution and make a plan to implement the solution. We move forward with celebration for successfully, as a team, resolving the issue. It is amazing how well this simple process works.

EXERCISE
COMMUNICATION

❤ Make a list all the things you love about your partner.

❤ Make a list of all the things you are happy about in your relationship.

❤ Identify an issue that you would like to improve.

❤ Identify several possible solutions that would remedy the issue.

❤ Prepare your Presentation.   Include the following components:

    ❤ What I love about my partner;
    ❤ What I am happy about in my relationship;
    ❤ Issue I would like to improve; and
    ❤ Several possible solutions that would remedy the issue.

❤ Rehearse your Presentation.

❤ Schedule a "Family Meeting" with your partner, when you can have uninterrupted time, in a quiet, pleasant setting or a public place.

❤ Present your Presentation.

❤ Be prepared for discussion and be open to many possible solutions.

❤ Choose the best solution and prepare a plan to implement the chosen solution.

❤ Celebrate your discussion and the pattern you've set for healthy communication.

Note: This exercise can be modified and used for any challenge or challenging relationship in your business life or personal life. We have found this formula very helpful in every area of life. By starting with the positive, we set the tone for a pleasant discussion and a favorable outcome.

WORKSHEET
COMMUNICATION

1. Love:

_____

_____

_____

_____

_____

_____

2. Happy About:

_____

_____

_____

_____

_____

_____

3. Issue for Improvement:

_____

_____

_____

_____

_____

_____

4. Possible Solutions:

_____

_____

_____

_____

_____

5. Prepare Presentation:
    Include:
        What I Love
        What I'm Happy About
        Issue for Improvement
        Possible Solutions

_____

_____

_____

_____

_____

6. Rehearse Presentation
7. Schedule a Meeting
8. Present Presentation
9. Discussion
10. Choose Solution and Plan to Implement
11. Celebrate

Ten Desirable Communication Modes

Below are two lists, together they contain ten words that describe our communication style within our relationship. Listed is what we always do and what we strive to be:

Always:
- Honest
- Kind
- Loving
- Considerate
- Respectful
- Helpful

Strive To Be:
- Straight-Forward and Bold
- Harmonious
- Fair
- Generous

Ten Communication Modes to Avoid

Never:
- Angry
- Mean
- Rude
- Complain
- Aloof
- Disrespectful
- Raise Voice

- Dishonest
- Secretive
- Argumentative

Fortunately, we don't need a lot of communication rules because we genuinely love and care for each other. It is easy to be respectful and kind when you love your partner as much as you love yourself. We each contribute more than 100% to the relationship and we are always looking out for the best interest of each other. We have created a win-win-win situation. It is a win for me, a win for Craig and a win for our relationship. It is great to be on a winning team!

Chapter Ten
Transform Your Relationship

"Life has taught us that love does not consist
in gazing at each other,
but in looking outward together in the same direction."
--Antoine de Saint-Exupery

So, what do you think? Do you want a passionate loving relationship? How bad do you want it? Would it be worth your time to make an effort to improve your relationship?

It all boils down to this: If you continue doing the same things, you will continue to have the same outcome. Are you a talker or a doer? Are you willing and ready to take action? We get what we give in our relationship and we guarantee that the outcome, a passionate loving relationship, is worth every bit of effort. Are you willing to make changes to improve your relationship?

In order to get where you want to go, you must first determine where you are at. The following exercise will be helpful to assess and determine where you are at and where you want to end up.

EXERCISE:
SCORE YOUR RELATIONSHIP

💜 Without assistance or feedback from your partner, on a scale of 1-10, rate yourself and your partner for each of the following categories and rate your relationship with an overall score. A score of 1 is very poor, a score of 5 is average, and a score of 10 is excellent. Rate yourself and your partner. Ask your partner to do the same.

<u>Category</u>	<u>Me</u>	<u>My Partner</u>
Unconditional Love	_____	_____
Communication Skills	_____	_____
Follow-Through on Commitments	_____	_____
Generosity	_____	_____
Affection	_____	_____
Playful	_____	_____
Compassion	_____	_____
Integrity	_____	_____
Honesty	_____	_____
Trustworthiness	_____	_____
Money Management	_____	_____

Rate your relationship's overall level of success _____

This is not a contest, there is no winning score. This exercise is about perception. How do you perceive yourself, your partner and your relationship?

Compare with your partner. It will be interesting to note the difference in perception. Which areas need improvement? In which areas were your scores significantly lower or higher than your partner's scores? This is an excellent exercise to generate honest discussion.

Chapter Eleven
Epilogue

"The most wonderful of all things in life
is the discovery of another human being
with whom one's relationship has a growing depth,
beauty and joy as the years increase.
This inner progressiveness of love
between two human beings
is a most marvelous thing;
it cannot be found by looking for it
or by passionately wishing for it.
It is a sort of divine accident,
and the most wonderful of all things in life."
--Sir Hugh Walpole

• *Mishael*

Two decades later we look forward, with great excitement, to our Friday night dates when we have dinner out or dinner at home on the back patio at the Patton's Café. The excitement still feels similar to years ago when I drove to the Pink Flamingo Hotel to meet Craig and begin our weekends of fun in the wine country. Now on our dates we celebrate a week of hard work and discuss our successes and challenges.

Why is it that we are so consistently excited to see each other? Why is it that our love is so grand, so dynamic, and so delightful? I had just celebrated my 40th birthday when I met Craig. We had been around and we were both very clear about what we did not want in a relationship. We read, studied, researched and explored, and together we determined what we wanted in our relationship and then we got busy and created it. As I look back, I know that spending time together and consciously building the foundation for our relationship has contributed to our success.

We recognize that we have got a good thing going on; we truly treasure and take care of our relationship. This translates into taking good care of each other. Every day we look for ways to show our love, to please and pleasure each other with surprises and kind words and gestures.

You get what you give, definitely holds true in our relationship. Without holding back, I give a lot, and the result is that I receive a lot. It takes two willing players who play full out and each give more than 100%. An extreme attitude of giving, with the right partner, results in extreme receiving.

One component of our relationship success is that we have maintained a healthy balance of time apart and time together. We each have individual, personal areas of interest that the other doesn't share and we encourage independent time apart.

Craig is an active volunteer in Desert Sheriffs Search and Rescue (DSSAR), Craig has found his niche and loves his DSSAR activities. He is Vice President of the Board of Directors and there are meetings and trainings several times a month that result in a significant time commitment, in addition to being on call twenty-four/seven. I support, encourage and celebrate Craig's DSSAR commitment because it fulfills him. When he returns from training or a search, I always prepare a "Hero Dinner". Truthfully, the menu is no different than what I would normally prepare, but it is my way of saying and demonstrating love and recognition for his hard work and contribution to the community.

I have a passion for books, libraries and book stores. Though Craig has little interest in spending hours in a library, he certainly doesn't object to me having a wonderful time there because he knows it results in extreme happiness for me.

There are many other examples I could share, but for us, it has worked well that we have maintained our individual identities and activities. Our time apart, doing individual activities, seems to enhance and strengthen our relationship. Although we benefit from individual time apart, we certainly have many activities that we enjoy together.

We love to take our kayaks out on the ocean; we go out of Oceanside Harbor, in southern California. Though it is great exercise, we consider it a romantic activity because being on the ocean brings back memories of the infamous trip from Marina del Rey to Catalina Island. We typically paddle to the Pier, take a break, have a snack and do "kayak meditation", we close our eyes and drift around for a bit before paddling back to the marina. The ocean is different every time we go out, the swells out there are fantastic and sometimes we see dolphin. Being out in nature fulfills us.

We enjoy preparing meals together. Everything is more fun when we do it together. Teamwork is an amazing component of a loving relationship. For us every meal is a party or fiesta, we often light candles. Each time we sit to dine we celebrate being together, being in love and sharing a meal.

I love to prepare healthy food and present it beautifully. I sincerely believe that food prepared with a loving attitude contributes to health and wellness. When we have family or friends with us, we present meals with the same level of love and enthusiasm. The best part is when my dear husband clears the table, does the dishes and cleans the kitchen.

We live in La Quinta, California, twenty miles east of Palm Springs in the Coachella Valley where the hiking trails are awesome. We enjoy day hikes with a snack party mid-hike.

Sometimes we spend a day under the umbrellas by the pool, conversing, reading and napping. In the midst of our busy lives, a relaxing day with my best friend is very desirable. In the summer time, floating in the pool at night and star-gazing is a dreamy desert activity that we find to be very romantic.

In all of our activities, whatever it might be, there is a lot of enjoyed silence; conversation is not always a necessary component, a loving heartfelt glance or smile will suffice. When we share activities our intention is always to create a romantic adventure. Romance is everywhere when your intention is to make it happen.

The AWC Women

Unfortunately we have lost contact with Kristen, Estela and Bev. Gail married in 1999, retired in 2001, continues to live in Santa Rosa and enjoys six grandchildren. Kathleen married in 2003, works for a non-profit agency in Santa Rosa and, with her husband, has one grandchild. Trudy has two wonderful sons and teaches computer design at a Santa Rosa area high school. We look forward to reuniting with the AWC women when we are in Calistoga for book signing events.

Wrap Up and Conclusion

Here's the big secret! It all starts with you; no one can do it for you. Whether your partner participates, or is even aware of what you are up to, you can impact and improve your relationship. It is all out there and waiting for you. Make the choice to begin the journey. Envision the outcome you want, begin thinking about and talking about what you want, then take the steps to transform your relationship.

Visit our website at www.LoveHealsHearts.com. Contact us and let us know about your relationship challenges and successes. Sign up for a coaching session or workshop.

Remember, Franklin P. Jones said, "Love doesn't make the world go 'round. Love is what makes the ride worthwhile." Here is to living your life fully and participating in an awesome passionate and loving relationship. Through love, may you discover happiness and fulfillment in all areas of your life. Good luck to you in creating the relationship of your dreams.

About the Authors

Mishael grew up in the Eugene, Oregon area and Craig grew up in Manhattan Beach, California. They both had been married, divorced, were single for many years and had grown children when fate brought them together on a sailboat charter from Marina del Rey to Catalina Island. They reside in La Quinta in the sunny southern California desert.

Mishael and Craig decided to share their story because they believe the world needs love. They have created their company, Love Heals Hearts, to promote their books, movies, products and services to spread the energy of love and light around the planet and out into the Universe. For more information visit their website at www.LoveHealsHearts.com.

(Photograph by: Chris Miller, Imagine Imagery)

www.ingramcontent.com/pod-product-compliance
Lightning Source LLC
Chambersburg PA
CBHW020251290526
45784CB00003B/1207